GANDHI & ART
AND
OTHER ESSAYS

Texts, Visuals and Performance

RAMAN SINHA

INDIA • SINGAPORE • MALAYSIA

ISBN
Paperback ISBN 979-8-89556-506-3
Hardcase ISBN 979-8-89556-507-0

To Bulbul & Anna —

'My friend, with you to live alone,

How much better than to own

A crown, a sceptre, and a throne!'

CONTENTS

Preface   7

1. Interdependence and Autonomy in Indian Arts   9

2. Pre-Modern Indian Art, Society and Culture   16

3. East Meets West: Mughal Miniature & European Art   25

4. Iconography of Tulsidas   42

5. Poetry in Ragas or Ragas in Poetry?   61

6. Bindadin Maharaj and the Evolution of Kathak   78

7. Gandhi & Art   94

8. Indian Classical Music: Adapting or deteriorating   187

9. Other in self: An Indian Doctor in China
    & A Chinese Hawker in India   192

10. Self in Performance: Rituparno Ghosh as Chitrangada   202

Bibliography   213

Acknowledgements   229

PREFACE

This collection of essays brings together works originally written for various national and international academic seminars over time. While the majority of the essays were composed in English, the first two were initially presented in Hindi and are now translated into English for the first time. Each essay reflects the intellectual engagement and contemplations sparked by the themes of the seminars, which, when viewed retrospectively, seem to have been influenced by a timeless vision of the interconnectedness of art as propounded in the *Vishnudharmottara Purana*.

The *Vishnudharmottara Purana* contains a profound dialogue in which Vajra seeks to understand the art of sculpting deities. Markandeya, in his wisdom, explains that mastering sculpture requires a foundational understanding of painting. Vajra, intrigued, then asks about painting, only to be told that true comprehension of painting is impossible without an appreciation of dance. Markandeya continues, illustrating that dance cannot be fully understood without knowledge of music, which, in turn, depends on the ability to grasp the essence of singing. This profound interdependence of artistic disciplines resonates deeply, revealing the essence of art itself. It is a principle that I find not only fascinating but also lamentable in an era dominated by over-specialization. Achieving such holistic understanding remains an aspirational ideal, and these essays represent my humble attempt to engage with a small part of it.

It is my hope that readers will find moments of resonance within these pages---- sparks that inspire their own reflections on the intercon nected nature of creativity. How much of my yearning for this artistic unity will speak to them, or what meanings they might draw, is something I cannot predict. As the poet so wisely said, "The connoisseur sees the pearl, not the diver's unsuccessful efforts!"

—Raman Sinha

Centre for Indian Languages

Jawaharlal Nehru University

New Delhi.

1

INTERDEPENDENCE AND AUTONOMY IN INDIAN ARTS*

"All Indian art is a throwing out of a certain profound self-vision formed by a going within to find out the secret significance of form and appearance, a discovery of the subject in one's deeper self, the giving of soul-form to that vision and a remoulding of the material and natural shape to express the psychic truth of it with the greatest possible purity and power of outline and the greatest possible concentrated rhythmic unity of significance in all the parts of an indivisible artistic whole."[1]

There is a lot of similarity in the ways in which pre-colonial Indian arts translate aesthetic experience into art forms, moreover there is also an extraordinary similarity in the nature of aesthetic experience itself. Kapila Vatsyayan rightly pointed out that, "Classical Indian architecture, sculpture, painting,

---

1   Sri Aurobindo, The Foundations of Indian Culture, Sri Aurobindo birth centenary library, volumes 14, Sri Aurobindo Ashram, Pondicherry, 1972, p.241

*   This is a translated version of a paper presented at Gujarat University, Ahmadabad, on 24th December 2011

literature (Kavya), music and dancing evolved their own rules conditioned by their respective media, but they shared with one another not only the underlying spiritual beliefs of the Indian religio-philosophic mind but also the procedures by which the relationships of the symbol and the spiritual states were worked out in detail."[2] In Bharat's Natyashastra, the detailed description of the plot, character, acting type, *Vritti, pravritti, dharmi,* songs, instruments and dance has actually been explained only for the sake of permanent emotion (sthayee bhav) and means and skill for inducing Rasa. The technique of Indian music, like Indian drama is also based on detailed analysis of each individual unit striving for a *sthayee bhava* leading to Rasa. Indian composers also use the same ideas and techniques as Indian playwrights. Just as an Indian poet or playwright presents a *sthayee bhava* with a single plot to express a particular interest, similarly an Indian musician also chooses a particular raga to express a particular interest. Like various types and methods of dialogue, soft, sharp, pure tone is envisaged, the aalap, sthayee and antara (Pallavi, anupallavi and charanam in Carnatic music) of the raga are reminiscent of *sandhis* in drama, and the movements of the ragadari are like various abhinaya forms. Similarly, the twenty-two *Shrutis* mentioned by music theorists are like gestures in dance or like words in poetry, and despite the independent existence of gesture and word, their role is recognized only in the context of overall composition of the poem or dance. As it is commonly believed that seven swaras are made from twenty-two Shrutis only and as Sarang Dev has said, "The smooth, resonant, self-compounding sound produced after the Shruti is called

---

2 Kapila Vatsyayan, Classical Dance in Literature and the Arts, Sangeet Natak Akademi, Delhi, 2nd Edition, 1977, p.8

'Swara'."[3] Each swara signifies a certain feeling or state of mind, which is classified on the basis of its relative importance, like in *Narada Samhita*, the seven swaras have been seen as the seven parts of unconsciousness—sa (Shadaj) is considered to be the soul, Re (Rishabh) is considered to be the head, Ga (Gandhar) is considered to be the arm, Ma (Madhyam) is considered to be the chest, Pa (Pancham) is considered to be the throat, Dha (Dhaivat) is considered to be the lips and Ni (Nishad) is considered to be the foot. These tones are also considered to be sensitive to the seven basic elements originating from the seven chakras of the body.

Reflecting on Indian sculpture, Sri Aurobindo says, "The more ancient sculptural art of India embodies in visible form what the Upanishads threw out into inspired thought and the Mahabharata and Ramayana portrayed by the word in life. This sculpture like the architecture springs from spiritual realisation, and what it creates and expresses at its greatest is the spirit in form, the soul in body, this or that living soul-power in the divine or the human, the universal and cosmic individualised in suggestion but not lost in individuality, the impersonal supporting a not too insistent play of personality, the abiding moments of the eternal, the presence, the idea, the power, the calm or potent delight of the spirit in its actions and creations. And over all the art something of this intention broods and persists and is suggested even where it does not dominate the mind of the sculptor. And therefore as in the architecture so in the sculpture."[4]

---

3   Sarangdev, Sangeet Ratnakar, Sangeet Karyalaya, Hathras, first edition, 1964, p.20
4   Sri Aurobindo, ibid, p.229

Indian dance, like Indian poetry, music and sculpture, also seeks to convey timeless, impersonal feelings and transcends the physical plane through the medium of human form. The plots that Indian dancers present are not the raw material of literature but are mature literary works; the music that plays along with them is an inseparable part of the structure of the dance; In fact, what the dance interprets in movement, the music captures in sound, and their postures and gestures are those which were created by Indian sculptors. Actually, there are two important aspects of Indian dance: Nritta (based on rhythm through graceful movements of the body) and acting. Dance depends on music and rhythm for its existence, whereas the acting aspect depends on narrative or songs sung for its expression. The acting aspect of dance was originally conceived by Acharya Bharat as an inseparable part of drama. In Natyashastra, he has mentioned dance as an aspect of drama and in the same sequence, the human body was analyzed from tip to toe— on the one hand, to explore the possibilities for movements of each organ of the human body, on the other hand, the usefulness of the movements of these organs in showing a particular emotional state has been considered.

It is not surprising that in any book on Indian art, while talking about any particular art form, the art critic hardly able to limit himself to that, just as while talking about dance, discussion on literature and music becomes inevitable; Similarly, while considering sculpture, drama, music and painting, the topic of dance definitely comes up in some form or the other. The concept of Rasa in painting has been taken from the vision described in Natyasastra and similarly, in the books of sculpture, the discussion of dancing idols of various Gods and Goddesses or the mention of symbolism of hand gestures is based on the *angika abhinaya* of Natyashastra. It is the interdependence of arts that gives a unique dimension to Indian art, but art forms also have their own autonomy which they do not give up easily and even when they are influenced by other art forms, they do it on their own terms, as per their own grammar. If we consider raga-mala pictures or the role of words in Indian classical music, it became clearer.

The concept of raga mala was already developed in literature and music before it was used in painting. To understand the transcendental characteristics of music, apart from a sound form, a corporeal and divine form was needed, for this reason *dhyan* (meditation) was invented. Among the Ragamala paintings found so far, the oldest *dhyan* is considered to be of Hanuman, whose period is believed to be between fifth to twelfth century. In Dattila or Narada's Ragasagar, we see forms of initial *dhyana*, in which the raga has been portrayed in a corporeal and divine form. Similarly, this tradition continued in Matang's Brihaddeshi, Narada's Sangeet Makarand, Sarang Dev's Sangeet Ratnakar, Meshakarna's Raga Mala etc. In all these collections, an attempt has been made to put into words the musical specialties of the raga - to highlight the divine character of the raga, to give technical information about it and to use poetry to define the expressed rasa. Klaus Ebeling, who did the authoritative work on Raga Mala, opines that here poetry did not remain a mere companion of music, rather the importance of the divine aspect of Raga, the importance of which had been established in many ways by the musicians, was disregarded and its human aspect—

human weakness and human emotions were emphasized.[5] This is a demonstration of how arts maintain their autonomy while blending with other art forms. Ananda Coomaraswamy, while working on the Hindi text of Raga Mala, had also realized that "like the pictures they represent given situations Raga-Mala, like paintings, texts represent certain situations and associations, or in other words, a given character in a given psychological environment, corresponding to the ethos of the several Ragas and Raginis. These emotional situations are similar to those recognized by the rhetoricians, so that in the Ragmalas the classification of heroines (Nayika-bheda), phases of love in union (*Samyoga*) and love in separation (*viraha*), and times and seasons play a large part: and some of the pictures, e.g. the *Abhisarika* type of *Madhu-Madhavi* Ragini referred to below, could at the same time be used in illustration of the works of the rhetoricians. As literature, the Ragmala poems are in fact related to such poetry as the *Rasikpriya* of Kesav Das and Satsai of Bihari: and like these works, they are far more than descriptions."[6] This act, which is *far more than description*, is also a kind of demonstration of the autonomy of the art. If we pay attention to the role of words and literature in classical music, it is easily discernible that words of *bandish* for notes have not become acceptable because of their literary value, but their ability to be adapted as a sound unit in musical composition is the sole reason for their selection. It is also a proof of the autonomy of music that the literariness or words of the composition is considered less important as Pandit Lalmani Mishra pointed out that, "If we want to upgrade the

---

5   Klaus Ebeling, Ragamala Painting, Ravi Kumar, Paris, 1973, p.28

6   Anand Coomaraswamy, Hindi Ragmala Texts, in Journal of the American Oriental Society, vol. 43, 1923, p.396

importance of words in Khayal music, then definitely we will degrade its high position. I myself have done such experiments many a times and have made other musicians too to do so but the results were not satisfactory. Late Pandit Vishnu Digambar started the practice of imparting education by intoning the words of saint poets in classical music, he himself used to sing the compositions of saint poets during last phase of his life. His fellow disciple Sangeet Chudamani Pandit Vinayak Narayan Patwardhan Continuing his tradition, has also published many such compositions (*Bandishes)* in his books, but in the classical music circles, these are called raga-based bhajans and the *Bandishes* have not got the prestige what old *khayals* had. In fact, it is correct to say to some extent that if the literature of these verses is sung as per the demand of Khayal style, it has to be distorted and consequently their literary beauty will be lost and the meaning will be distorted and If their literary beauty and meaning is preserved than the singing of Khayal style cannot be accomplished."[7]

A similar scenario of interdependence and autonomy can be discerned in almost all the art forms in India.

---

7   Lalmani Mishra, Sangeet aur Samaj, Madhukali Prakashan, Bhopal, first edition 2000, p.14

2

PRE-MODERN INDIAN ART, SOCIETY AND CULTURE*

The images of the contemporary society and culture reflected in the medieval Indian art forms seem to have been created by the mutual conflict and coordination of folk and classical at one level and Hindu and Islamic perception at the other. This conflict and coordination can be seen taking place in the arena of two types of organizations. The first organization is of the state and the second is of religion. The Delhi Darbar had a central position in medieval India. It was not just the center of political power, but it was also a centre where parameters were set for all the patterns of what we call culture, from language, literature, architecture, painting, music to clothing, food, drinking, manners and fashion. It is believed that the norms accepted in the Delhi Darbar were ultimately consolidated and spread all over India through the Amir-Umra, regional Darbar representatives, Jagirdars and Zamindars. The famous historian

* This is a translated version of the 10th Rahul Sanskrityayan memorial lecture at Triveni, Delhi on 9th April 2004.

Percival Spear, who worked on the twilight of the Mughal Empire, has written that, " The Mughal court, so long as it lasted, was the school of manners for Hindustan. From the time of Akbar it had much the same influence upon Indian manners as the court of Versailles upon European. ...From Bengal to Punjab and as far Madura in the south, Mughal etiquette was accepted as the standard of conduct and Persian was the language of diplomats and the polite. Forms of address, the conventions of behaviour and to a large extant ceremonial dress, approximated to the standards of Delhi. Even the Marathas felt its subtle and all-pervading influence, and the Jats were proud to decorate a replica of a Mughal palace at Dig with the plunder they had carried from Delhi."[8] Mohammad Hussain Azad writes at one place in *Aabe Hayat* that "When Ahmed Shah Durrani's army destroyed Hindustan and Fugan[9] saw the condition of Delhi, he went to meet his uncle Iraj Khan in Murshidabad where his star was ascendant. At this time, whenever a person from Delhi went anywhere, people believed it as if a fairy had arrived and his way of behaviour, mannerism and etiquettes were considered as a criterion of politeness and decency."[10] How canons were formed and spread in the pre-modern India can be understood with an example from the arena of music. There were two classes of musicians in the courts, one was called *Huzuri* and the other was *Darbari*. Musicians who could theorize and adept at compositions were called Hujuri. For their superiority in

---

8   Percival Spear, Twilight of the Mughals, Cambridge at the University Press, 1951, P 82–83

9   Renowned poet of Urdu:Shraf Ali Khan 'Fugan', death 1722

10 Muhammad Hussain Azad, Urdu Kavya ki Jeevan-dhara, Nagari Pracharini Sabha, Varanasi, First Edition 1979, P.112

qualities, thoughtfulness and creative skills, this class used to be present with the emperor every day. Artists like Tansen and Ramdas of Akbari Darbar belonged to this class. New types of Malhar and Kanadas were created by this class. This class also used to make new compositions in old and popular ragas. They also discussed their compositions among themselves and in this way new ragas were authenticated as *Taksali* or sealed form.

"The artists of the Hujuri class used to teach these *Taksali* compositions to those class of artists, which was called Darbari. These people used to be present in 'Darbar-i-Aam'. This class was considered lower than the *Hujuris*.

"Even in the court of the governor of the emperors, only those artists were valued who remembered the traditional Bandishes, hence the Bandishes created by the Hujuri class were publicized in the entire country."[11] This system continued till Mohammad Shah *Rangeela* (1719–1748). It was making of a paradigm for a court style. Actually, the category of folk and classical has been evolved in some form or the other since very beginning— there is a division of *Gandharva* and *Gaana* in Natyashastra in which *Gandharva* has its origin from Samaveda and Gaana has its origin from *Gandharva*. The listener mainly gets the benefit from *Gaan*. ... In Gandharva, note (*Swar*) and rhythm (*Taal*) are important... whereas Padas are important in Gaan.[12] Later, there a division between *Desi* and *Margi* happened, but as noted sociologist D. P. Mukherjee has noted, "The exchange between Desi and Margi styles continued continuously during the Muslim period. The

---

11   Sulochana Brihaspati, Darbar aur Sangeet, in Acharya Brihaspati, Sangeet Chintamani, bhaag 2, Brihaspati Publication, New Delhi, 19 87, p.229

12   Premlata Sharma, Sahaasras, Sahitya Akademi, New Delhi, First Edition, 1972, pp.112–116

opposition of conservative scholars was canceled by making the new court style equivalent to the ancient style. The courtly style became classical with 'Margi'."[13]

Meditating over Music in India— from Natyashastra to Sangeet Ratnakar (1231 AD)— was inevitably based on *Gram Murchhana* method but in the entire pre-modern period, with the establishment of Indraprastha School, *Muqam* method came at the center of discussion. Sulochana Brihaspati has written that "Muslims considered twelve independent swaras in the *Mandra, Madhya and Tar* octave, in which no Swara was considered to be a distortion of any other Swara. It was difficult for the Indians to believe in the existence of twelve swaras in the octave. This was a new thing, because they considered only seven notes in each scale (sthana). The agreement was made that by considering Shadaj and Pancham as fixed and the remaining five notes should be considered with two variations of it. Today what we call *Thata* or *mela* the Iranian people had the word *Mukam* for it... Due to the influence of Indraprastha, *Saptak* (octave) was replaced by *Ashtak* in India."[14] This was a sorts of paradigm shift which music theorists have considered as the biggest influence of Muslims on Indian music. In music legends, it has been marked as the victory of Amir Khusro over Gopal Nayak[15], but some music thinkers also say that, "Even if Muslims had not come to India, natural change would have shaped Indian music. Therefore, it would not be right to think that the system of raga classification promoted by Muslims completely changed the soul of Indian music. It is certain that with the

---

13 D.P.Mukherjee,Indian Music, Kutub Publishers, Pune, 1945, p.12

14 Sulochana Brihaspati, ibid, p.226

15 Ibid, pp.92–93

addition of Muslims system of classification, a non-Indian type of hybridization of ragas also became popular in India, new ragas also entered, but, it is sure that the new classification had established no connection with Indian *Rasa Shastra*. The result was that Sanyog, Viyog, Vairagya, Songs of devotion and bravery etc. started being sung in every raga indiscriminately."[16]

A similar dilemma is faced by the thinkers considering the pre-modern architecture when they find in Muslim architecture the overwhelming presence of Hindu motifs like Chakra, Padma, Purna Kalash, Shrivatsa, Swastika Gavaksha, Kirtimukha, Shatakon etc. — not only in the Mughal buildings but also in the buildings of the so- called conservative Delhi Sultanate. Whether this was used only for decorating purposes or it was the aim of assimilating their original symbolic recesses also?

Moreland pointed out two types of industrial activity during the time of Akbar: one centered on the state-protected factory and the other based on individual labour and private capital.[17] Sir Thomas Roe had seen Indian artisans working in state protected factories during the reign of Jahangir and Bernier during the reign of Shahjahan and Aurangzeb. Bernier has noted that, "Large halls are seen in many places called karkhanas or workshops for the artisans. In one hall embroiderers are busily employed, superintended by a master.in another you see the goldsmiths: in a third, painters: in a fourth, varnishers in lacquer work: in a fifth, joiners, turners, tailors, and shoemakers:

---

16   Acharya Brahaspati, Musalmaan aur Bhartiya Sangeet, Rajkamal Prakashan, Delhi, 2nd edition, 1982, p.11

17   W.H.Moreland, India at the death of Akbar, Macmillan and co.London, 1920, pp.186–187

in a sixth, manufacturers of silk, brocade, and fine muslins."[18] Craftsmen work here from morning till evening—passing their time in a calm and carefree manner. They do not care at all about improving the conditions of the place where they are born. A craftsman wants to make his son a craftsman, a goldsmith wants his son to be a goldsmith and a physician wants his son to be a physician. No one marries outside his profession, neither a Hindu nor a Muslim.[19]

Such *karkhanas* (factories) could be seen in every corner of the country, but the big factories were in Kashmir, Lahore, Agra, Ahmedabad, Fatehpur and Burhanpur. For the first time during the time of Akbar, it happened that the craftsmen were not recruited on the basis of their caste, religion, colour or region. Akbar's famous translation center was also located in this *karkhana* where Persian translation of Ramayana, Mahabharata, Simhasana Battisi and Bhagvat was done, and also beautifying the manuscript with illustration in Mughal miniature style. The emergence of the Mughal style is considered an epoch-making event in the history of Indian painting. It is true that the Safavid painters Mir Syed Ali and Khawaja Abdul Samad, who came from Persia with Humayun in India, and "continued the traditions of Turkistan," as noted art critic Ananda kumaraswami pointed out but soon they established their independent existence. Anyway, under the rule of the great Shah Abbas, Persian art was heading towards decline. One reason for its independence from the Persian art was that two-thirds of the Mughal painters were Hindus and like the Mughal emperors, Mughal art also soon

---

18   Ibid, quoted on page p.

19   Tripta Verma, Karkhana under the Mughals, From Akbar to Aurangjeb, Pragati Publications, Delhi, First Published, 1994, p.23

became Indian.[20] In another study, Kumaraswami considered Mughal art in comparison to Rajput art, a typical courtly art as he aptly announced that, "While Mughal art is a court art, Rajput is a folk art." He further elaborated it by saying that Rajput art has the same relation with the classical period of India as native (*bhakha*) poetry has with Sanskrit. In Rajput painting, like Bhakha poetry, there has been such a confluence of folk with classical traditions that it has become the culture of the entire country. In which the king and the farmer have equal share."[21] Here it is natural to remember Hazari Prasad Dwivedi, who at many places had considered the union of folk and classical as the basis of all-encompassing public practices (*lokdharma).*[22]

In the Pre-Modern period, as indicated at the beginning, artists received patronage from two power centers: first from the state like Delhi, Agra, Gwalior and second the religious sects like Pushti, Ramanandi and various sects of Sufis. It is also evident that both these power centers were not independent from each other but were mostly interdependent for their status and dominance. There was mutual conflict between these two power centres but it also became a center of coordination where folk and classical intermingled. It is true that Turkish and Persian were dominant languages in the royal courts but the native language was used in the Khanqahs of Sufis. Jayasi has mentioned in *Akharavat* that great Sufis were usually conversed

---

20 Anand Kumaraswamy,Introduction to Indian Art, Munshiram Manoharlal, Delhi, Second edition, feb 1969, pp.76–77

21 Anand Kumaraswami, Rajput Painting,Motilal Banarasidas, New Delhi, second edition, 1976, p.2

22 Hazariprasad Dwivedi, Hindi Sahitya ki Bhumika, Rajkamal Prakashan, New Delhi, edition 2010, p.115

in Hindi. The Khanqahs of Sufis also became the confluence of Indian and non-Indian singing styles.[23] It is also noted in history that not only Mansingh Tomar —who gave the royal status to a native language— was responsible for establishing Brajbhasha in the Akbari Darbar along with the singing art of Gwalior, but also in 1577 AD the summit of Akbar with Vitthalnath ji in Agra is also responsible for it.[24] It is also worth considering that why the duality of religion and erotica and *Ishq Haqiqi* (worldly love) and *Ishq Majaji* (unworldly love) were not considered dualities as such? Was it something in the sensibility of that era that poet Raskhan says: "Happiness is not experienced, without love the world knows./ Who is he talking about carnal happiness (Vishyanand), who is describing spiritual happiness (Brahmanand)".[25] And when another prominent poet Bodha clearly declares that, "worldly love is reality, /No one can find it without going beyond it."[26] So it becomes clear why master of erotic literature Acharya Keshavdas writes in praise of Bhakta Vitthalnath and aestheticist Bihari Satsai exhorts, "the reflection of whose fair body falling on dark-complexioned skin of Krishna turns it into a spark of green."[27] And the devotional prayer of Riti

---

23 Acharya Brihaspati, Musalmaan aur Bhartiya Sangeet, ibid, p.23

24 See, Harihar NIwas Dwivedi, Madhyadeshiya Bhasha, Vidyamandir Prakashan, Gwalior, Pratham sanskaran, 1955, pp.119–121

25 आनंद- अनुभव होत नहिं, बिना प्रेम जग जान। कै वह विषयानंद, कै ब्रह्मानंद बखान।। Vidyanivas Mishra, Satyadev Mishra(eds), Raskhan Rachnavali, vani Prakashan, Delhi, 1993, p.88

26 इस्क हकीकी है फुरमाया। बिना मजाजी किसी न पाया।। Vidyanivas Mishra(ed), Bodha Granthavali, Nagri Pracharini Sabha, Varanasi, Pratham sanskaran 1974, p.54

27 जा तन की झाईं परैं, स्यामु हरित-दुति होइ। Jagannath Das Ratnakar, (ed.),Bihari-Ratnakar, Tara book Agency, Varanasi, 1990, p.1

Shiromani Beni Kavi is expressed as "May Radhika shyam visit always in our heart lovingly in such a way."[28]

On the other hand, accomplished Sufi poet Jayasi is writing *Nakh Shikh, Ritu Vilap and Barahamasa*, devotee Surdas is composing *Sahitya Lahari* and Bhakta Nandadas is paying attention to the difference between various heroes and heroines in *Rasmanjari* and Bhakta Shiromani Tulsidas describes in *Barvai-Ramayana* the beauty of Sita in such a way : "That is, O friend, although gold is no less than Sita's body in colour, beauty and in giving pleasure, one big difference is that Sita's body is soft and gold is hard."[29]

The erotica of the Bhakta poets and the devotion of the erotic poets are the expressions of the same state of mind of the pre-modern world where the individual is seen to be in dialogue with the state or religion and the classical interacting with the folk, the native with the foreign and the tradition with experiments and innovations.

---

28   नित ऐसे स्नेह सों राधिका स्याम हमारे हिय में सदा बिहरैं। Ramchandra Shukla, Hindi Sahitya ka Itihas, Nagri Pracharini Sabha, Kashi, 1983, quoted on p, 169

29   सम सुबरन सुखमाकर सुखद न थोर ।सिय अंग सखी कोमल कनक कठोर। Ramnaresh Tripathi, Tulsidas aur unki Kavita, Pahla Bhag,Hindi Mandir Prayag, Pahla Sanskaran, 1937, p.206

3

EAST MEETS WEST: MUGHAL MINIATURE & EUROPEAN ART*

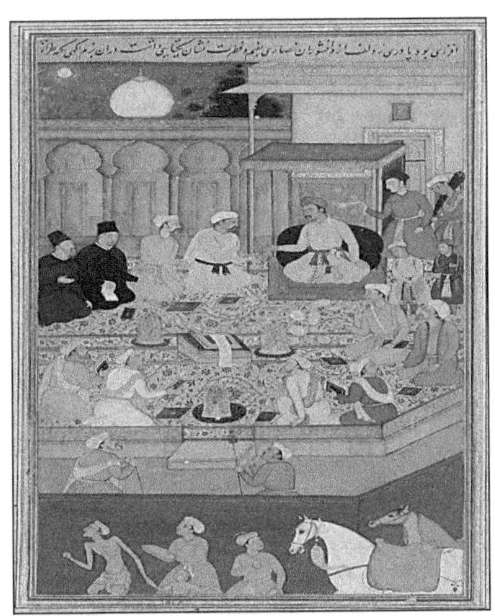

The cover page shows Mughal Emperor Akbar (r. 1556–1605) holds a religious assembly in the Ibadat Khana (House of Worship) in Fatehpur Sikri; the two men dressed in black are the Jesuit missionaries Rodolfo Acquaviva and Francisco Henriques. Illustration of the Akbarnama, miniature painting by Nar Singh, ca. 1605

*   This is a revised version of a power point presentation in a seminar on St Francis Xavier and the Jesuit Missionary Enterprise :Assimilations between cultures in Goa on 2nd December 2011

OH, EAST is east, and west is west,

And never the twain shall meet [30]

The Mughal painting...showed that it was still possible to found a new art on the basis of the old traditions: foreign influences were, not perhaps easily, but at last effectually, assimilated, and the result was a new and great art, which...is truly original.

—*Anand K. Coomaraswamy* [31]

The Mughal art came across European paintings, prints, engravings and other decorative arts in early 1570s. [32] One of the member of first Jesuit mission to the Mughal court (1580–1583), Anthony Monserrate noted the presence of European art on the wall of royal dining-hall at their arrival in Fatehpur sikri. [33] It is believed that the first European paintings that reached Akbar's court were large oil paintings of Mary, the mother of Jesus. Mary was a known figure in Akbar's court. She is the only woman mentioned by name in the Qur'an, and Akbar's mother was named Maryam, the Arabic form of the name Mary. This mission had presented a copy of Jesuits' Bible to Akbar that

---

30 Rudyard Kipling's Verse, Doubleday, page and company.inc, New York,1920,p.268

31 Anand K. Coomaraswamy,Art & swadeshi, Munshiram Manoharlal Pvt Ltd.second edition 1994,pp.79-80

32 The first wave of European prints dating from the 1540s must have arrived with Francis Xavier who was sent to India in 1542, or subsequently with fifty of his Jesuit brothers who joined him in Goa after 1555. Some of these mid-sixteenth century prints were probably acquired by the Mughal embassy to Goa in 1575. The second wave, dating from the latter part of the century must have arrived at the Mughal court with the three Jesuit missions, the first in 1580, the second in 1591, and the third in 1595.

33 Correia-Afonso, John, ed., Letters from the Mughal court: the first Jesuit mission to Akbar, 1580–1583, Bombay: Gujarat Sahitya Prakash, Anand, 1980, p76.

was Plantyn's Royal Polyglot Bible with illustration done by some Flemish painter of the school of Quintin Matsys (1466–1530) and P.Huys. It is reported that when Akbar received this Bible, *"he held them in his hands and publicly kissed them, and placed them on his head...."* A Jesuit priest observed Akbar's behaviour in following words: *removing his cap or turban, kneeling on the ground with great devotion, he prayed before the picture of Christ and of the Virgin, venerating thrice, once in our manner, the other in that of the Muslims and the third in the Hindu fashion, that is to say, prostrate, saying that God should be adored with every form of adoration.*[34] This Jesuit mission had also introduced some western paintings of post-renaissance period, especially Flemish art of Antwerp school and the work of Johann Sadeler (1550–1600), Hieronymus Wierix (1553–1619), Raphael sadeler (1555–1618) and Theodar Galle (1571–1633)— these were subsequently copied and adapted in Mughal miniature paintings and murals by the court artists of Akbar (r. 1556–1605), and later Jahangir (r. 1605–1627) and Shah Jahan (r. 1628–1657) at Fatehpur Sikri, Agra, Lahore and Delhi. In 1580, Akbar allowed Portuguese Jesuit priests from Goa to set up a chapel in his palace; there they exhibited two paintings of the Madonna and Child before a large and excited crowd. Douglas Galbi in his work, "Sense in Communication" describes this event in following words: "This one was a copy of the Madonna del Popolo, a *hodigitria* that Pope Gregory IX presented to a church in Rome in 1231. Ten thousand persons came in one day in 1602 to see the painting. A great Captain, "accompanied by more than sixty men on horseback," came to see the painting.

---

34   Mac lagan, Edward Douglas, The Jesuits and the Great Mogul, Burns, Oates & Washbourne, London, 1932, pp. 227–8

Madonna and infant Jesus, Mughal[35]   An European in Mughal India[36]   ca. 1590 Jahangir holding the picture of Madonna[37], circa 1620 A.D., National Museum, New Delhi

Although he had already seen other *hodigitria*, Akbar asked that the painting be brought to him. He kept it overnight in his "sleeping apartment," where his wives and children lived. Soon thereafter Akbar's mother requested that the painting be brought to her, and so did other socially and politically important persons. The painting became a crowd attraction and a performance piece."[38] Father Pierre Du Jarric describes this incidence in this way: *A great crowd of people had assembled in the palace yard in the hope of being able to see the picture...seeing that they would be able to satisfy so large a number of persons at one time, [the Jesuit priests] placed it where all could see it and publicly uncovered it. The moment it was exposed to view, the noise and clamor of the crowded courtyard was hushed as if by magic, and*

---

35 Madonna and infant Jesus,Mughal, (http://www.tribuneindia.com/2005/20051225/spectrum/main2.htm)

36 An European in Mughal India,ca. 1590 (http://www.tribuneindia.com/2005/ 20051225/spectrum/main2.htm http://collections.vam.ac.uk/item/O17478/watercolour -portrait -of-a-european/

37 Jahangir holding the picture of Madonna ,circa 1620 A.D., National Museum, New Delhi

38 http://www.galbithink.org/lessmore.htm

the people gazed on the picture in unbroken silence.[39] Subsequent Portuguese clerics as William Dalrymple noted, found that the gospel books brought by their predecessors had led to murals of Christ, his mother and the Christian saints being painted on the walls not only of the palace but also on Mughal tombs and caravanserais: *"[The emperor] has painted images of Christ our Lord and our Lady in various places in the palace," wrote one Jesuit father, "and there are so many saints that (...) you would say it was more like the palace of a Christian king than a Moorish one."*[40]

The Jesuit Priests presented to the Mughal court not only Christian paintings but some non-religious works like portraits of nobility, landscapes, woodcuts, silk and woolen tapestries, illustrated books, etc. Later, Flemish copper engravings were also introduced—it affected the current painting scenario of the Imperial Mughal Studio mainly in two ways: firstly some European painting and person found their ways directly into their canvas along with some biblical themes and secondly their style of presentation somehow changed. There are few paintings where European paintings are shown hung on the wall of the depicted palace and in some work European characters are independently delineated.

It is said that when Indian artists made copies and adapted versions of the western paintings, prints and engravings their subject-matter and the very grammar of their art gradually started changing. Not only Scenes from the life of Christ like Nativity, Adoration of Magi, Flight to Egypt, Crucifixion,

---

39 E. Denison Ross and Eileen Power (ed.) Akbar and the Jesuits, Tulshi Publishing House, New Delhi, 1979, p. 168.

40 https://en.qantara.de/content/what-muslims-and-christians-share-a-christmas-meditation

Deposition, Christ and the Apostles, and Christian saints, The Madonna and Child and Virgin Mary, European type winged angels or cherubs playing musical instruments, became popular subjects of their canvases and murals but the very prominent Mughal artists like Kesu Das, Basawan, Govardhan, Payag, Bichitra and Abu ul Hasan etc had started giving the prominence in their oeuvres, of never tested before aerial perspective and modeling, spatial depth and chiaroscuro effect, use of full faces and frontal poses, subdued colour of hazy landscapes and overall a kind of approach that may be called humanist. *The Madonna and Child* and *Virgin Mary* were very popular subjects in the Mughal court. A Madonna and Child by Kesu shows a very Baroque treatment of drapery and the tree. Scenes from the life of Christ like Nativity, Adoration of Magi, flight to Egypt, Crucifixion, deposition, Christ and the apostles, and Christian saints were depicted not only in the Mughal miniatures but also in the royal palaces. One scholar notes: *"European visitors to the palaces and tombs of the emperors of Mughal India ("Mogor" in Portuguese) between the 1590s and 1660s were amazed to find them prominently adorned with mural paintings depicting Christ, the Virgin Mary, and Christian saints executed in the style of the Late Renaissance. To their astonishment, they also discovered Mughal artists at work on large numbers of miniature paintings, exquisite jewelry, and sculptures of the same subjects – including many which were apparently even being used as devotional images."*[41]

---

41   Bailey, Gauvin A., Art on the Jesuit missions in Asia and Latin America, 1542–1773, University of Toronto Press, Toronto, 1999, p. 112

Crucifixion, Keshu Das[42]

A crucifixion, with the Virgin and Saint Anne[43]

The Deposition from the Cross[44]

Mirat-ul-Quds (The Mirror of Holiness), one of the most precious illuminated manuscripts of Lahore Museum and a masterpiece of Akbar's time, consists eleven miniatures depicting the life of Christ in the Mughal mannerism with an influence of European traditions and Christian Symbolism. The exposure to European artistic traditions began to blend in with the Mughal style and typical Indian miniature repertoire of court scenes, portraits of royalty, hunting parties and musical soirees were started changing. European characteristics like aerial perspective, spatial depth, chiaroscuro effect, use of full faces, frontal poses, subdued colour and overall so called humanist approach were started emerging evidently in the work of prominent Mughal

42 Crucifixion, Keshu Das http://www.flickr.com/photos/22955235@N00/ 1239254680/in/set-72157600028124617

43 A crucifixion, with the Virgin and Saint Anne, from Akbar's court, c.1600; in the collection of the Aga Khan Museum http://www.columbia.edu/itc/mealac/ pritchett/00routesdata/1500_1599/akbar/europeanart/europeanart.html

44 The Deposition from the Cross, Unknown, c.1598, Mughal, Watercolour,Gold, ink on paper, Victoria and Albert Museum, London http://www.conniemadson.com/artmovements/09%20 islamic%20and%20mughal%20art.html

artists like Kesu Das, Basawan, Govardhan, Payag, Bichitr and Abu ul Hasan etc. Their portraits of dervishes, Sufis and philosophers need special mention in this regard. It is also worth noting what Som Prakash Verma

| The Birth of Christ[45] | c.1775 Adam[46] | c.first half of the 17th century, The Last Super[47] |

formulates: "The Mughal artist, under the influence of Renaissance humanist movement in art added a new chapter in Indian art which is neither a direct continuation of the pre-Islamic Indian traditions and nor explicitly Persian. The Mughal painting, eclectic in character, evolved with the interaction of various traditions, predominantly Indian Persian and European. The context of naturalism, scientific perspective, and chiaroscuro—contrasts in light and shade in Mughal painting

---

45   The Birth of Christ ,c.1775,National Museum,New Delhi(no.58.20/281)

46   Adam , c.first half of the 17th century, Chester Beatty Library, Dublin. The last Supper, School of Shah Jahan, Bharat Kala Bhavan, Banaras, Acc, no, 690 Mhttp://www.cbl.ie/cbl_image_gallery/collection/list.aspx?collectionId=2

47   The last Supper, School of Shah Jahan, Bharat Kala Bhavan, Banaras, Acc, no, 690 M

is the gift of humanism as practiced by the European artists of Renaissance."[48]

Madonna with Infant Jesus[49]

Madonna and Christ c18th Century, Pahadi style[50]

One of the most prominent painters of Akbar's atelier and also one of the Jahangir's favourite early artists was Kesu Das. He is well known for his highly skilled copies of European engravings; especially of Minerva, St Jerome[51], the story of Joseph[52], St. Matthew and the angel & Crucifixion[53]. As it was pointed out by one critic, "His picture 'St Mathew and the angel', executed in 1587–8, was based on a print of an engraving by Philip

---

48 Som Prakash Verma, Interpreting Mughal Painting, New Delhi, Oxford University Press, second Impression 2011, p103

49 Madonna with Infant Jesus Unattributed, 17th century, Mughal, Prince of Wales Museum of western India.
http://www.chapatimystery.com/archives/homistan/postcolonial_skins.html

50 Madonna and Christ c18th Century, Pahadi style,
http://www.mullocksauctions.co.uk/lot-41541   india_%E2%80%93_mughal_painting _of_ christ_c18th_century.html

51 See Amiuna Okada, Imperial Mughal Painters, Paris, 1992, pl.100, p.97

52 See, Milo Cleveland Beach, The Grand Mogul: Imperial Painting in India 1600-1660, Sterling and Francine Clark Art Institute, Massachusetts, USA, 1978

53 See, Illustrated in J.M. Rogers, Mughal Miniatures, London, 1993, pp.44-68

Galle after Martin van Heemskrek 'St Mathew the Evangelist' and is almost European in character. In his copy, the Mughal painter has successfully delineated the folds in the robes of the saint and the facial expression in his figure.Kesavdas's picture 'Joseph telling his dream to his father' (c.1600), based on an engraving by George Pencz, dated 1544, is another outstanding

St. Matthew and the angel[54]   Minerva[55]   Kesu Das Minerva[56], Basavan

Mughal copy of a European work revealing the artist's full control on European technique and style. In his picture of St Jerome adopted from Mario Cartaro's print of an engraving of Michelangelo's Noah from Sistine chapel, Kesavdas's understanding of the subject is explicit in the rendering of the muscular modeling close to the style of Michelangelo. Bailey observes that Kesavdas has excelled here. In fact, the pulsating

---

54   St. Matthew and the angel, Kesu Das;
     http://en.wikipedia.org/wiki/Saint_Matthew

55   Minerva, Kesu Das, http://www.columbia.edu/itc/mealac/pritchett/00routesdata
     /1500_1599/akbar/europeanart/europeanart.html

56   Minerva, Basavan, c.1600, http://www.columbia.edu/itc/mealac/pritchett/00routes
     data/1500_1599/akbar/europeanart/europeanart.html

flesh of his image is more Michelangelesque than the Italian engraving he copied."[57] Besides Kesu, Basawan was another insightful painter of his time and his skill and independence in copying European engravings and Christian iconography is very clear in two drawings published in Imperial Mughal Painters[58] Basawan's Minerva is quite different from the original in some radical way. The treatment of the young woman's cloak, which rises above her shoulder and her hand position, is depicted very different from the original.[59]

Traditionally Minerva is shown with a spear in her hand but Basavwan portrays her with a string instrument, perpaps Rabab or veena in her hand but as in original she is shown here also standing in front of books. It is rightly emphasized that "In the context of the rendering of symbolic images, Basawan, a prolific painter of Akbar's court, was the foremost. He showed a fascination for European emblematic picture/figures, and exhibited considerable ingenuity in their adaptation by introducing some alterations suitable to the taste of the Mughal

---

57   Som Prakash Verma, ibid, p114

58   Amina Okada, Imperial Mughal Painters, Paris, 1992, nos. 89 and 90, p. 89

59   An European-style Minerva stands on a pedestal, holding a string instrument and chain, confronted by a baby and surrounded by various articles including a book and a ewer, a later inscription to the bottom of the drawing reads Ustad Basawan or 'Master Basawan', laid down with pale green and pink margins illuminated with gold flowers and gold, red and blue margins with blue rule on blue tinted paper, with gold wildlife on a leafy ground, a short note below, lower margin an inscription contemporary with the signature, verso with four diagonal lines of flowing nasta'liq signed Muhammad Husayn [Zarrin Qalam] similarly margined, ruled and mounted, small localized areas of repair. Miniature 7 × 3½in. (17.8 × 8.9cm); Folio 14½ × 9 3/8in. (36.8 × 23.8cm.) A note in the lower margin, presumably intended for the binder, translates 'Facing the [painting] of the woman holding a baby in her arm'. Minerva. Mughal India, Drawing ascribed to Basawan, Calligraphy by Muhammad Husayn Zarrin Qalam, Circa 1600. Album leaf, brush drawing on paper.

court."[60] No wonder this discretion made Mughal painting open towards European works to influence them quite creatively. For example, in the painting *Jahangir Preferring a Sufi Shaikh to Kings* has ample evidences of European influence, as illustrated in the naked cupids and the image of King James I of England, with the haloed emperor sitting on an hourglass throne. It depicts the ruler as favoring spiritual power over worldly power and moreover to hallow him artist tried to give him some kind of metaphysical authority. It is also to be noted that, "The symbolic representation of God in human form in the Mughal School is almost certainly derived from European pictures connected with the episode of Crucifixion, where God's portrayal in a full-fledged human form emerged during the fifteenth century. An application of this European symbol in the delineation of the emblematic pictures of the Mughal emperors is significant, since it suggests their own link with divinity. Undoubtedly, the representation of God in human form in imperial Mughal painting was a bold step by the artists. We know that in Islamic paintings, there is always a restraint in this regard, albeit without any inhibition in case of the portrayal of the prophets. The application of European symbols, namely, the halo, angels, cherubs, and God the father in Mughal portraits added an air of spirituality to the picture..."[61] The influence of European technique of painting is also very much evident in one of the areas where the use of stereoscopic perspective and Sfumato were applied and this is certainly a decisive break with the earlier techniques of Persian painting of the court where figures near the horizon differ little in size

---

60   Som Prakash Verma, ibid, p.109

61   Som Prakash Verma, ibid

from those in the foreground and where objects appear stacked, one upon another. Mughal artists initially tried to cope with this new found perspective in a curious way,

Jahangir Preferring a Sufi Shaikh to Kings[62]

detail from the painting[63]

Jahangir, Bichitr, Triumphing over Poverty[64]

for example in this miniature— *An Angel Conversing with a Group of Europeans*— which is a free paraphrase of an engraving by the German artist Georg Pencz (c. 1500–1550), the Indian artist tried to render the domed building with linear perspective, without much success. However he did a better job at using aerial perspective, in which the intensity of the colors decreases as distance increases as we know the deliberate blurring of a line or contour to make an object seems to disappear in the distance, or to add a soft-focus effect to a face or body in the foreground.

---

62 Jahangir Preferring a Sufi Shaikh to Kings Bichitr (act. 1615–50) India, Mughal period. Opaque watercolor, gold, and ink on paper. Smithsonian Institution, Washington D.C. http://resobscura.blogspot.com/2011/02/jahangirs-turkey-early-modern.html

63 detail from the painting created in 1618 by Bichitr for the Mughal emperor Jahangir(1569-1627). Here we find the strange juxtaposition of James I and VI of England (1566-1625)

64 detail from the painting Emperor Jahangir, Bichitr, Triumphing Over Poverty, ca 1620-1625 http://collectionsonline.lacma.org/mwebcgi/mweb.exe?request=record ;id=37429;type=101

In the Khamsa, this technique is used in conjunction with another technique, that of painting distant landscape in pale blue in order to create the appearance of distance through gradual shifts of colour from dark to pale tones towards the horizon. Many of the engravings found in Mughal possession excel in

| The King Carried Away by a Giant Bird [65] | An Angel Conversing with a Group of Europeans[66] | Shapur Brings Khusrau News of Shirin[67] |

the technique of modeling – using light and dark tones to depict the direction of light in order to conjure up the illusion of three dimensions. This is seen best in the modeling of cloth.

---

65   The King Carried Away by a Giant Bird – The Story of the Princess of the Black Pavilion, by Dharmdasa From the Khamsa of Nizami, Painting on paper, British Library Or. 12, 208, 1593-95, 30 × 19.5 cms http://asianart.com/articles/minissale/5.html

66   An Angel Conversing with a Group of Europeans, Mughal; c. 1610, Miniature: 17.9 × 9.5 cm, http://www.davidmus.dk/en/collections/islamic/materials/miniatures/art/6-1981

67   Shapur Brings Khusrau News of Shirin ,Dharmdasa,From the Khamsa of Nizami, f. 52a,Painting on paper British Library Or. 12,2081593-95,30x19.5 cms http://asianart.com/articles/minissale/4.html

European engravings provided clear models of the principle of establishing the direction of light. Although there are several examples of Mughal artists rendering the light and shade of folds of cloth in the Khamsa manuscript, the most impressive study appears in the work *Shapur Brings Khusrau News of shirin* here, the curtains of the tent show the Mughal artist's masterful use of the European technique of modeling and principle of establishing the direction of light and a new interest in using colours to depict light and shade, rather than solely as areas in an overall chromatic structure. Since Indian miniature painting had a long and living tradition of assimilating different streams of conventions related with Jains, Buddhists, Rajputs and Persian origins; the new element of European traditions also got assimilated with passing of times. The eclectic tastes of the Mughal rulers also played a crucial role as it gave rise to the use of various sources for artistic persuasions among the court painters. Alongside illustrations of a few classics of Iranian literature, they also encouraged or commissioned the copying of great illustrated works of Indian culture like of *Ramayana* and *Mahabharata*. No wonder they were very proud and possessive about their artists and their patronage were extended to them across the cast, creed or religion. It is clearly reflected in the off quoted incidence of Thomas Roe with Jahangir— "a picture of a friend of mine that I esteemed very much, and was for curiosity rare, which I would give His Majesty as a present. When the moment for making the presentation finally came, the Emperor took extreme content, showing it to every man near him: at last sent for his chief painter, demanding his opinion. The fool answered he could make as good, whereat the King turned to me, saying my man sayeth he can do the like and as well as this: what vow? A wager was set, the painting handed over to the imperial painter, and on the day appointed the King sent for me, being hasty to triumph in his workman, and showed me six pictures, five made by his man, all pasted on one table, so like that I was by candle light troubled to discern which was which for that at first sight I knew it not, he (the Emperor) was very merry and joyful and cracked like a northern man."[68] It is also true that imitation is not simply reproduction rather in the process of imitating, it becomes hybrid especially when the artist is not a 'fool'!

Recent scholarship tries to explain the art produced in Mughal-Court during Jesuit mission as interactive and hybrid: "Most art and architecture on the Jesuit missions was produced with the more or less willing participation of indigenous communities, and almost all of it can be described as a hybrid. Sometimes the admixture contained more European ingredients than indigenous ones, as was generally the case in Japan and Paraguay. Elsewhere, as in eighteenth –century China or Mughal India, the indigenous element prevailed, relegating European style or ideals to the details. In every case, however, the merging of two alien traditions inspired new solutions and ideas, often of great originality. It demonstrates the creative potential of cultural convergence, with its blending, confluence, overlap, and ambivalence —art that is considerably more than the sum

---

68   W.Foster, (ed.) The Embassy of Sir Thomas Roe to India 1615–19, Munshiram Manoharlal
     Publishers, Delhi, 1990

of its parts."[69] This gestalt of cultural convergence, as we have noticed questions the very formulation of beginning lines of the Ballads of East and West : "OH, EAST is east, and west is west, / And never the twain shall meet" as not only they meet but they react and interact too.

---

69 Bailey, ibid, p.5

4

ICONOGRAPHY OF TULSIDAS*

In Indian tradition a poet is generally considered to be a seer or a person with divine vision—it is by experiencing the divine that man becomes a *ṛṣi* (seer) or a *kavi* (poet). In his ādikāvya (the first poem) Vālmīki describes his creative process:

> *Vālmīki utters the primal metrical line when he witnesses an act of violence in the forest. He then has a vision of the god Brahma, the ultimate repository of the Sanskrit tradition, and sinks into meditation. Gaining knowledge of Rama's 'full story, public and private' he renders it as Kavya by means of the meter and 'elegant speech' just produced through Brahma's will.*[70]

It is no coincidence that Nābhādās considers Tulsidas to be a reincarnation of Vālmīki for the redemption of mankind in this perverse *kaliyuga* (age of strife).[71] In premodern times, Tulsidas

---

70 Quoted in Sheldon Pollock. Language of the Gods, Permanent Black, 2006, p77

71 कलि कुटिल जीव निस्तार हित,बाल्मीक "तुलसी" भयौ। त्रेता काब्य निबंध करिवसत कोटि रमायन। इक अक्षर उद्धरैं ब्रह्महत्यादि परायन॥ भक्तमाल, नाभादास, (सं) सीतारामशरण भगवानप्रसाद रूपकला, तेजकुमार बुक डिपो लि., लखनउ, 2009, पृ. 756

* This is a revised version of a Power Point Presentation in the 12th International Conference on Early Modern Literatures in North India at University of Lausanne, Switzerland 0n 16th July 2015.

was well-known, since biographical works of the poet were plentiful, and he was largely perceived and accepted as a devotee of Rāma and a seer-poet almost unequivocally.[72] Even if we leave aside these biographies and survey how he was perceived in visual media, our conclusions would not be very different.

Tulsidas in visual media

From the seventeenth century onwards, the portrayal of Tulsidas in visual media was largely uniform and indeed quite similar to

Figure 1 Tulsīdās: A young Vaishnava Saint. Prahlad Ghat, Varanasi. Courtesy Gosain Tulsidas by Viswanathprasad Mishra.

Figure 2 Tulsīdās: An old Vaishnava Saint. Sankata Ghat, Varanasi. Courtesy Gosain Tulsidas by Viswanathprasad Mishra.

---

72 see 'Tulsi charit' of Raghubardas; 'Mool gosaincharit' of Benimadhav Das; Tulsi sahib's 'Aatmacharitra', see also hagiographical work like 'Bhaktamal' or its commentary of Priyadas or comments of Vaisnavdas or Nagridas in 'Padprasang mala' or 'Do sau Bavan Vaisnavan ki Varta'

oral portrayals. The first portrait that has survived is considered to date to around 1608 CE (Fig. 1). It is claimed this portrait was made in the house of Pundit Gangaram Joshi of Prahalad Ghat, where Tulsidas was supposedly staying at the time recovering from a serious illness. Ranchorlal Vyas, who claims lineage to pundit Gangaram Joshi, published a monograph on Tulsidas in 1915 in which he also incorporated this painting in monochrome. According to Vyas, the portrait was made by an artist from Jaipur under the tutelage of Emperor Jahangir (1569–1627). The artist asserted his copy- right on this painting since, according to him, it was registered under his name. Later, it would be widely edited, beautified, copied, revised, and circulated. Kāśī Nāgarī Pracārinī Sabhā first enlarged it, had the 'anemic appearance' of its subject corrected by specialist artists and published it in *Tulsī Granthāvalī* (the collected works of Tulsidas) in 1923. However, a statement in the third volume of *Tulsī Granthāvalī* says that the published portrait was brought from the noted art col- lector and connoisseur Rai Krishna Das later. Gyanmandal Karyalaya published it in monochrome and the editors of the reputed Hindi magazine *Madhuri* published it in colour. According to the collector Rai Krishna Das, this is one of the two oldest paintings of Tulsidas. The other one, he explained, is in the collection of Bharat Kala Bhavan in Kashi. He emphasized the fact that the style of building shown in the Prahlad Ghat Portrait doesn't seem so old; that the architectural style developed much later after the rule of Mohammad Shah (1719–1748).[73] A more important painting of Tulsidas is Sankata Ghat Portrait (Fig. 2).

---

73   quoted in Vishwanathprasad Mishra, Gosain Tulsidas, Vani Vitan Prakashan, Varanasi, 1965, p 314

This painting belongs to the family of the mahant Radhavallabha Sharan of Sankata Ghat in Varanasi and according to him, as reported by Vishwanathprasad Mishra, it has been in their family's custody since Shahjahan's time (1628–1658). Radhavallabha ji also emphasized that Rai Krishna Das had taken the portrait to him for supposedly closer scrutiny; in fact, he got it copied after reworking it— Tulsīdās's beard was shaved and the setting was changed by the famous painter of Mughal tradition, Ustad Ram Prasad. There is also a painting of Tulsidas in the Mayashankar Yagyik collection, in which he is portrayed as a typical Vaishnava saint. One of the five obligations (*pañcasaṃskāra*) of a Vaishnava, as set out in the *Padma Purāṇa*, is to bear ornamental tilak (sectarian marks) on twelve pre-scribed parts of the body. In this painting of Tulsidas, all but one of these tilak are prominently displayed—one, on the right abdomen, is hidden due to his posture in profile. It is evident that the painter wanted to emphasize Tulsīdās's Vaishnava identity very prominently. As Vishwanathprasad Mishra speculated, it seems that there were two original pictures of Tulsidas—one in middle and one in old age.[74] The first tradition of iconography is based on the painting in the Kishangarh col- lection (Fig. 3) in which Tulsidas is portrayed as a middle-aged Vaishnava saint with long hair and beard, tilak, sacred thread, kaṇṭhī mala (necklaces/rosary worn by Vaishnava), and sumaranī (meditating beads). The originating painting of the second tradition of iconography is SGP (Sankata Ghat Portrait, Fig. 2), in which Tulsidas is depicted as an old saint with white beard bearing all Vaishnava identity marks. But there is also a third

---

74 Ibid,p.315

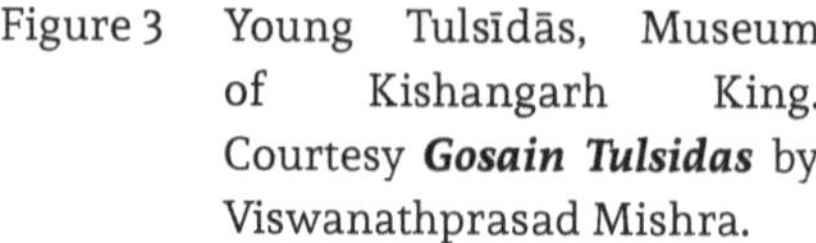

Figure 3 Young Tulsīdās, Museum of Kishangarh King. Courtesy **Gosain Tulsidas** by Viswanathprasad Mishra.

Figure 4 Tulsīdās reciting Rāmcaritmānas in an audience. Kiṣkindhākāṇḍa, Late Mughal. American Institute of Indian Studies, Gurgaon, Haryana, India

tradition in which Tulsidas is portrayed as old and clean-shaven, as in the golden-syllable Ramayana (Svarnākṣarī Ramayana) of Ramnagar, Varanasi. This illustrated manuscript was commissioned by the then king of Kashi, Sri Udit Narayan Singh (1783–1835). It took eight years (1796–1804) to complete and was valued at around one lakh and sixty thousand rupees. Tulsidas is portrayed in the manuscript as quite old and clean-shaven. He appears quite frequently in this manuscript and here (Fig. 3.4) is satin padmasana (lotus posture) with kaṇṭhī mala reciting his Rāmcaritmānas in front of a well-to-do gathering. The artist of this manuscript, Sri Ramcharan, appears to be trained in Mughal miniature painting. Ananda Coomaraswamy has categorized it as 'Mughal influenced post-Rajput miniature painting. Later this style was called 'Popular Mughal style.'[75]

Figure. 5   Tulsīdās with his disciples. Uttarakāṇḍa, Pahari, Mughal Art Network.

Figure. 6   Tulsīdās with a disciple. Hanuman Temple, Tulsi Ghat, Varanasi, U.P. India.

Another painted manuscript of Rāmcaritmānas was commissioned by Maharaja Sawai Ram Singh II (1835–1880) of Jaipur and again Tulsidas is portrayed prominently. There are 134 original paintings created between 1857 to 1864 for this manuscript. The final miniature of this manuscript is a depiction of Tulsidas himself (Fig. 5) seated on a throne reciting his magnum opus to a group of his fellow devotees, sitting on the floor. Here Tulsidas is depicted with beard and long hair, like his devotees around him. Other portraits of Tulsidas exist, such as the Tulsi Ghat Portrait, which was once considered to be very old and discovered late and, if we are to believe Rai Krishna Das, was 'done by a modern artist and totally artificial.' This is the only portrait of Tulsidas that is not in profile and

---

75   Ananda Coomaraswamy, Rajput Painting, vol.1, Motilal Banarasidas, New Delhi, 1976, p.1

has some resemblance in style with Sikh art (Fig. 6). Another portrait of Tulsidas is worth mentioning here, first published in Lon- don and later circulated in India. The fauna and flora, and the posture and age of Tulsidas, portrayed in this picture is very similar to the Kashi Ghat Collection. Features in this painting— the kamaṇḍal (water-pot), sacred threads, hair and beard style, glance perspective, riverbank—all suggest that either this or the

Figure 7   Tulsīdās on the river bank I. Bharat Kala Bhavan, BHU, Varanasi, U.P. India.

Figure 8 Tulsīdās on the river bank II. Gita Press, Gorakhpur, U.P. India.

paintings already discussed are copies of the other. Another portrait, which first appeared in the Tulsī Ramayana published by Khadagvilash Press, Bankipur, in 1889 CE, is credited as having been discovered by Dr. George Abraham Grierson (1851–1941). This is the only portrait where Tulsidas is depicted sitting in vajrāsana, a yogic sitting posture. The oil painting in the Rai Krishna Das collection (Fig. 7) has become over the years the most popular and considered authentic, though Rai Krishna Das never revealed its source. It seems that it was a reworking of an older picture and later on this painting was itself retouched, reconstructed, and reworked in various ways. In issuing a commemorative stamp of Tulsidas, the Indian post office adopted this portrait as its only source.[76]

The picture that appears in the Gita Press publication on Tulsidas (Fig. 8) is also largely based on this portrait.[77] It can be easily observed that the Gita Press artist, B. K. Mitra, had simply refor- mulated the Rai Krishna Das collection portrait in such a way to make it more 'real' and so consequently more 'popular' for commercial consumption. It can be considered a measure of success of this reworking that most of publications since have used it as the most standard iconography of Tulsidas. Gita Press has standardized and to some extant deified the icon of Tulsidas in all its publications. Later statues of Tulsidas installed in Hindu temples further made him more like a deity than a poet.

The Satya Narayan Tulsi Manas Mandir was built in Varanasi in 1964 as a memorial to Tulsidas and is a landmark in this regard since we hardly find any temple commemorating a poet or poetry in general. This magnificent temple not only houses a marble statue of Tulsidas and a jhanki (tableau) of wooden figures depicting scenes from his life. It also features engravings on the walls; frescos and the full text of the Kashiraj

---

76 Stamp was issued on 01/10/52 and this was one of the stamps of the first emissions printed by Photogravure in India and thus an important landmark in the evolution of Indian stamps. Biographical sketches portrayed on the stamps along with a couplet from each one of them are given in the succeeding pages. Vertical in design and measuring 1.6" X 0.95" the stamps are printed on all-over 5 pointed multiple star watermark paper- Perforation 14: Set 160. (http://www.indianpost.com/viewstamp.php/Issue%20Date/year/1952/TULSIDAS(Accessed 30 October 2018).

77 Gita Press has started using portraits of Tulsidas for its publication in a big way after its hugely popular 1938 Manas Ank of Kalyan.

edition of Rāmcaritmānas. The marble statue depicts Tulsidas in abhaymudrā (fearless posture). The tableau, which shows him continuously reciting Rāmcaritmānas, is another example of perception of him as a saint-poet.

Another temple in which Tulsidas is prominently displayed is Manas Mandir in Tulsi Peeth Seva Nyas, a religious and social service institution based at Janki Kund, Chitrakoot, Madhya Pradesh. Tulsi Peeth was established by Guruji Rambhadracharya on 2 August (Tulsi Jayanti Day) in 1987. The white-marble Manas Mandir temple, constructed in 2008, is situated at the entrance to the site, which incorporates several buildings and has a statue of saint Tulsidas in the centre. There is another,

Figure 9 Tulsidas in trance. Chughtai Museum, Lahore, Pakistan.

Figure 10 Tulsidas in Manikarnika Ghat. Life of the Medieval Saints, West Wall of Hindi Bhavan, Shantiniketan

larger-than-life-size, statue of Tulsidas inside the temple and three-dimensional paintings depicting different episodes of the Rāmcaritmānas in- scribed on the walls. In 2011 the Manas Darshan, an exhibition of moving models showing various scenes from the Rāmcaritmānas, was opened to the public and the statues of the poet unveiled.

Statues are very common for popular iconography but require some kind of likeness with the subject since it is an art form that is essentially realist in nature. Statuary presupposes a kind of eminence of the subject and its location of installation is also crucial to understand its areas of influence. Statues of Tulsidas are installed in Hindu temples and are made of marble, stone, wood, clay, and so forth. These statues, like his paintings, do not resemble each other in their outer physical appearance but what is common among them is their saintly persona and non-materialistic ambience.

Just as the figurative aspect of the painting lost its centrality in modern portraiture, Tulsidas began appearing in a very subjective way. In 1925 Abdur Rahman Chugtai (1897–1975) conceived Tulsidas (Fig. 9) in a way that is very similar to the portraits of Chaitanya Mahaprabhu, usually chiseled by the artists of the Bengal School. Chugtai was at the time very much influenced by the work of Abanindranath Tagore (1871–1951) and this work testifies it.

Another example of the modern depiction of Tulsidas can be found in the murals of Shantiniketan by Binod Bihari Mukherjee (1904–1980). The mural *Life of the Medieval Saints* (Fig. 10) is considered to be one of the largest murals of con- temporary India painted using the buon fresco technique.

It was executed on three walls of the Hindi Bhavan of Visva-Bharati in Shantiniketan between December 1946 and April 1947. Gulammohammed Sheikh observes:

The western wall is full of action with a dramatic image of Tulsidas in dialogue with an enigmatic character, probably Narhariyananad. The towering image of the Goswami stands in a performative gesture of supplication to an equally tall man holding a serpentine staff in one hand and gesticulating in animated exclamation with the other The Rising flames between the two protagonists indicate the location of Manikarnika ghat by the holy Ganga where the devout desire to die. A panorama of the busy Banaras Ghats surrounds the two. On the left, in a conglomeration of houses and shops, a daily drama unfolds; imbued with the rituals of death. The compatibility of life with the ritual of death enmeshed in a philosophical under layer is represented with a degree of dispassionate engagement. Or are we being led to follow the sadhu's view of samsara (world of mortals)?[78]

Whatever the case may be, it is certain that Tulsidas is not treated here like the earlier iconography of him as someone concentrating silently on the isolated bank of Ganga or Saryu, away from the hustle and bustle of the everyday life. Rather, he is shown very much in the midst of events and historical time.

Another example of modern treatment is K. K. Hebbar's rendering, in which Tulsīdās's life story is illustrated without any 'larger than life approach.' He is depicted in two scenes in the reproduced plate (Fig. 11) firstly it seems in the background of plague-ridden neighbourhood leaving, he is making his point clear to Rahim and secondly thus refusing Akbar's invitation

---

78 Gulammohammed Sheikh, Ruminating on Life of the Medieval Saints, by Benodbehari Mukherjee, The National Gallery of Modern Art, Delhi, date and page no. not mentioned.

Figure 11　Tulsidas with Rahim. Tulsidas: Hebbar's Narration in Lines.

to grace his court in such trying situation to Rahim. Hebbar made explicit his desire to illustrate the saint's life in 'simple lines,'[79] and his renderings illustrate how a poet struggles and over- comes various kinds of hurdles in life to achieve greatness.

Tulsidas in verbal media

There are three dramatic episodes that are said to have occurred in Tulsidas's life that have attracted the most vivid depictions among iconographers. The first episode relates to his wife Ratnāvalī, the second his encounter with the emperor, and in the third, the Lord Siva himself hails Rāmcaritmānas above the Vedas and Puranas. All three episodes may have first appeared in the Bhaktamāl commen- tary of Priyādās (1712)[80] and later,

79　K.K.Hebbar,Tulsidas,abhinav publications,Delhi,1989,(Acknowledgements

80　Sriseetaramsharan bhagwanprasad roopkala, Shreebhaktamal and Priyadas pranitt Tikka-Kavitt, Tejkumar book depot pvt.Ltd, Lucknow, 2009.

as Mata Prasad Gupta believes, incorporated in Bhavānīdās's Gosāīṁ Carit and Benīmādhav Dās's Mūl Gosāīṁ Carit.[81]

The question of fact or fiction aside, these episodes have great potentiality for dramatic impact—no wonder they constitute the most poignant material for any narrative of Tulsidas in any form. In his commentary, Priyādas describes the first dramatic episode thus:

He (Tulsidas) had great love for his wife. Without asking his leave, she went to her father's home, and he forgot all about himself, and hastened there too. She was greatly ashamed, and went away in anger, saying, 'Have you no love for Rama? My body is but a framework of skin and bone.' When he heard these words it was as it were the day break; he felt compunction and left her and went to the city of Kashi.[82]

This story became so convincing over the years that no narrative of Tulsidas— comic book, film, play, painting, novel, or poem—is considered authentic without incorporating it in some way.

Tulsidas in performative media

Poems about Tulsidas have been very popular in classical, folk and popular music over the years; but adopting his life or episodes from his life as subject matter in a form like viraha is a new phenomenon. Ramkripal Yadav's *Wife's Taunts Enlighten the Husband*, a music album of viraha, is one such example of a performative narrative that is structured effectively on the first dramatic episode in Tulsīdās's life. Priyadas's version of the second episode, The Emperor Visits Tulsidas, goes like this:

---

81 Mata Prasad Gupt, Tulsidas, Lokbharti Prakashan, Allahabad, 2002, p.78.

82 Cited in Madan Gopal, Tulasi Das, The Bookabode, New Delhi, 1977, p.113

The Emperor of Delhi sent an offer to fetch him... they spoke so courteously that he agreed and went. He arrived before the king, who received him with honour, gave him an exalted seat, and said in gracious tone: 'Let me see a miracle; it is noised throughout the world that you are master of everything.' He said: 'It is false; know that Rama is all in all.' 'How is Rama to be seen?' he said, and threw him into prison. He prayed within himself: 'O gracious Hanumana, have pity upon me.' That very moment thousands upon thousands of sturdy monkeys spread all over the place, clawing bodies, and tearing clothes, and great was the alarm. They broke open the fort, wounding the men, destroying everything; where could one fly for safety? It seemed as though the end of the world had come. Then his eyes were open by this taste of a sea of calamities, and the king cried, 'Now I wager all my treasure; it is he only who can save me.' The king came and clasped his feet: 'If you give me life, I live: pray speak to them,' he told the king, 'Better watch the miracle a little.' The king was overwhelmed with confusion. Then he stopped it all and said to the king: 'Quickly abandon this spot; for, it is the abode of Rama.' So the king quitted the place and went and built a new fort, and to this day anyone who abides there falls ill and dies.[83]

The same episode is described in Dās's Mūl Gosāiṁ Carit:

The king of Delhi requested the sage to show a miracle. Tulsi refused to oblige and was put in jail. The monkeys of Hanuman now assembled in the palace. They tore the clothes of the queens who were now exposed. They threw the king on the ground. There was terror in the palace. The saint was now released. The king asked for forgiveness. And Tulsi was sent away, with all honours, in a palanquin.[84]

---

83 Quoted in Madan Gopal, ibid, pp.114-5. (Tr.F.S.Growse)

84 दिल्लीपति बिनती करे दिखरावहु करमात। मुकरी गए बंदी किए कीन्हे कपि उतपात।।
बेगम को पट फारेऊ नगन भई सब बाम। हाहाकार मच्यौ महल पटको नृपहिं धड़ाम।।

Over the years, this episode has unfailingly caught the imagination of painters, film directors, comic book writers, and others.

Particularly in comic books, the narratives are more or less authoritative in nature as compared to novels and fiction in general. Comic books present their subjects as true stories—multiplicities of voice are not encouraged. For example, Amar Chitra Katha and Wilco both present this second dramatic episode in Tulsīdās's life in a way that is supposed to be convincing for readers. Selecting from a plethora of earlier tales, legends, and stories, they arrange the material to suit the 'taste' of their reading public.[85]

In the twentieth century, depictions of Tulsidas moved from static, two-dimensional forms to a dynamic interpretation of his life through film and performance. Most narratives of Tulsīdās's life have been adapted from premodern hagiographical works such as the Gautam Candrika or the Mūl Gosāī Carit. The Gautam Candrika describes Tulsīdās's persona and daily routine thus:

Tulasi (sic) would get up very early in the morning and spend some time singing songs, giving discourses or writing. He would then bathe in the Gan- ga, do Sandhya and, with a composed mind, as laid down, offer prayers. Af- ter this, he would offer water to those who deserved it and arghya (offering of water, flowers and uncooked rice) to the sun. With due ceremonies, he would offer leaves of bel tree to Vishwanath, tulasi leaves to Bindumadhav. Afterwards, he would enter the cave of Hanumana and offer fruits to gods. Then Tulasi would recite the

---

मुनिहि मुकुत ततछन किए क्षमाऽपराध कराय। विदा कीन्ह सनमान जुत पीनस पै पधराय।। Quoted in Mata Prasad Gupt, ibid, pp. 63–64

85 Tulsi Das, Madan Gopal, The Bookabode, Appendix-ii, p.73

whole of Adhyatma Ramayana and eat what others gave him, or what he got by begging. He would put on the ochre-coloured clothes. He had a tuft of hair, the sacred thread and a rosary.[86]

There are five biopic films in Hindi on the life of Tulsidas—made in 1939, 1954, 1964, 1972, and 2013. Others have been made in other Indian languages like Marathi (1939), Bangla (1950), Gujarati (1972), and Telugu (2012).

The first biopic film, Sant Tulsidas[87] is made in the tradition of devotional melodrama. This is one of the founding genres of Indian cinema and, as film critic Rachel Dwyer points out, 'the devotional films are often set outside brahmanical religion or question some aspect of it, and celebrate the introduction of vernacular language into worship.'[88] The dramatic pivot of the film revolves around Tulsīdās's realization of his life's vocation after being scolded by his wife amidst howling winds and a river flood. This is the turning point in his life and it caught the imagination of film-makers thereafter. He becomes an ascetic and settles down in Benares where his magnum opus Rāmcaritmānas outrages the Brahmanical clergy, until that point sole proprietors of the wisdom of Sanskrit texts.

---

86 Gulammohammed Sheikh, ibid

87 Produced by Jayant Movietone and directed by Jayant Desai, with music by Gyan Dutt and Vishnupant Pagnis, cinematography by Krishna Gopal, and dialogue by Pundit Indra, this film was released in Hindi and Marathi simultaneously in 1939. Songs were sung by Vasanti and Ram Marathe, who also acted in the film. The lead actors were Vishnupant Pagnis (who played Tulsidas), Leela Chitnis (Ratnāvalī), and Keshavrao Date (Baṭeśvar Śāstrī). 20 Dwyer (2007), p. 65.

88 Filming The Gods,Routledge,London and New York, First Indian Reprint 2007,p.65

A second film, Tulsidas,[89] was released in 1954. This critically acclaimed film[90] was technically much superior to first film. Its music compositions were a noted high, especially casting songs sung by Mohammad Rafi and songs like 'Kahan Chhupe Ho Raja Ram,' 'Hey Mahadev Meri Laaj Rahe,' and so on. The third dramatic episode of Tulsīdās's life—Siva's hailing of Rāmcaritmānas—was vividly highlighted in this film.

Next came Goswami Tulsidas, released in 1964[91] This film was largely in the style of films with a mythological theme; Tulsidas is portrayed reciting Sanskrit verses about Ram, inviting the wrath of kaliyuga, who instructs Kāmadeva to incite him with lust so that he abandons his vocation, marries Ratnāvalī, and devotes all his time to her. The film, however, fails to authentically make its point as its narrative was dependent on so many 'suspension of disbelief.'

Eight years later, a fourth biopic appeared. Sant Tulsidas[92] was made, supposedly, only for believers since Tulsidas interacts with Siva, Hanuman, and other mythical characters and at the same time transcends historical timelines and talks with saints like Kabīr with equal ease. This film was released in Hindi and Gujarati simultaneously in 1972.

---

89   Produced by Ratnadeep Pictures, directed by Bhalchandra Shukla and Harsukh Bhatt,,Music by Chandra Gupta, Lyricis by Gopal Singh Nepali, Star casts were Mahipal, Shyama, Raj Kumar, Dulari, Sunder, Ramesh Sinha, Uma Dutt,

90   Filming The God,ibid,p.86

91   Directed by B.K.Adarsh, the star cast of this film is inclusive of Shahu Modak, P.Kailash, Tuntun and Jaymala in leading roles, music direction by S.N Tripathi, written and screenplay by Adarsh, dialogue by Naval Mathur and B.D. Mishra.

92   Directed and produced by Pundit Bhalchandra and acted by Rekha Chauhan, Dalpat, Vijay Dutt, Shahu Modak, B.M. Vyas, released in 1972.

The latest film on Tulsidas is Goswami Tulsidas, released in 2013.[93] This film is more realistic in tone and far more technically superior than all earlier films. The traditional episodes of Tulsīdās's life are presented in such a way that the contemporary viewer may empathize with the poet in his distress and sublimation.

Beyond film, Tulsidas is presented in other performative arts such as television series and theatre. One episode of the Indian TV series Upanishad Ganga titled *'Glory of Human Birth'* depicts Tulsidas in a much more undeified form.[94] Shekhar Sen wrote, composed, directed, and acted in *Goswami Tulsidas*, a mono-act musical play depicting the entire life sketch of the poet using mostly his work. The play begins as Tulsidas arrives on earth for a day and tells his story. It's a story of how an orphan beggar boy becomes the greatest poet in India. Shekhar Sen presents Tulsidas as a social reformer who rebels against the exploitation of poor and ignorant people by the Sanskrit-literate priestly class and writes the Ramayana in a local language. This 120-minute-long drama was presented in fifty-two musical parts. These musical parts were not mere accompaniment—they were the very structure of the play. The play was presented in 1998 on the eve of 501st anniversary of the poet's birth.

The iconography of Tulsidas in narrative forms differs from its non-narrative forms. Portraits are like snapshots; narrative

---

93 Produced by Matcha Srinivasa Rao and Screenplay- direction by Allani Sreedhar.The films lyrics & dialogues are written by D.K.Goel & Music composed by Shashi Preetam. In this film 'Goswami Tulsidas' is played by actor Sunil Sharma and Pooja Baluti is playing his wife Ratnavali's role and Vindu Dara Singh is playing Hanuman.

94 This twenty-third episode of the series was directed by Chandraprakash Dwivedi and produced by Chinmay Mission, broadcast on DD National in 2012.

presupposes a story. The story of Tulsidas has been told in verbal media like biography, vārtā (written hagiography), novels, and poems and also in visual media like film, theatre, TV series, paintings, sketches, comic books, and so on. These narratives can be classified further into two categories—premodern and modern—based on their treatment of the subject and the timeline. Most hagiographical and biographical works treat Tulsidas as having some kind of supernatural power and this is the main characteristic of premodern iconography. In contrast, some modern renderings of Tulsidas insist upon his human aspects in a realistic form; films like Tulsidas, Sen's solo play *Goswami Tulsidas*, Dwivedi's *Upanishad Ganga* episode, and Yadav's *viraha*. Not covered in this chapter, we may add to this list two novels—Amritlal Nagar's Manas ka Hans and Rangeya Raghav's Ratna ki Baat—and Nirala's long poem Tulsidas. All these works portray Tulsidas as a creative person who evolves through his hardships in life. Despite this contrast in interpretation, modern presentations have continued premodern tendencies to mythicize this subject, as it is said, 'more the things change, the more they remain same!'

5

POETRY IN RAGAS
OR RAGAS IN POETRY?*

Some poetry communicates like literature; some like music or painting. The poetry which communicates like literature uses literary devices, whereas poetry communicating like music or painting uses the non-referential devices of these media. But sometimes the boundary blurs and the relative importance of the component parts defines a new sort of category altogether. Hence Bharatmuni (2nd century) defines *gāndharva* as a composition involving *svara* (notes), *tāla* (rhythm) and *pada* (words), and differentiates it from *gāna* on the ground that *gāndharva* gives more importance to *svara* and *tāla,* whereas *gāna* is comprised primarily of *pada*-centered compositions.[95] *Svara* and *tala* are musical devices, whereas *pada* is a literary one. Abhinavagupta (950–1030 C.E.) further elaborates this

---

95 "गान्धर्वं त्रिविधं विद्यात् स्वरतालपदात्मकम्" Dr.R.S. Nagar (ed.), Natyasastra of Bharatmuni, with the commentary Abhinav Bharati, vol.4, 28/11, Parimal Publications, Delhi, 1998,

* This paper was presented in the 11th International Conference on Early Modern Literatures in North India at Indian Institute of Advanced Study, Shimla on 6th August 2012.

distinction in his *Abhinavabhāratī,* stating that the importance of *pada* in *gāna* is of one type whereas in *gāndharva* it is of different type. *Svara* and *tāla* are important in *gāndharva* and since it is impossible to present them without any vehicle, *pada* as a vehicle becomes useful. That is why Abhinava says *pada* is a felicitator (*anubhavaka*) of *svara* and *tāla*.[96]

Another category that had been developed in Sanskrit in this context is *rāga* poetry or *rāgakāvya*. It can be traced at least at the time of Kohal (3rd century), who defined and classified it as a subcategory of *uparūpaka.* This was later quoted by Abhinavagupta in *Abhinavabhāratī.*[97] Abhinavagupta cites two examples of this subcategory—*rāghava-vijaya* and *marīcavadham*—and informs us that the former work was based on raga *thakkā,* whilethe latter work was composed in raga *kukubh.* Basically, *rāgakāvya* was meant to be enacted with dance, but it can also be sung as a song. It is composed in a single raga or multiple ragas, and *dhruvak* or a combination of *sthāī* and *antarā* is also used in it. Jayadev's *Gītagovinda* is a pioneer work in the tradition of *rāgakāvya,*[98] but before the *Gītagovinda,* the *Caryāpada* of *siddha* poetry (8th to 12th century) also provided an indication of the ragas appropriate to it. The *Caryāgītikośa,*

96　"किन्त्वन्यथा तस्य (पदस्य) प्राधान्यं गानेऽन्यथा च गान्धर्वे। तत्र हि स्वरतालौ प्रधानम्। तौ चनाधारौ न शक्यौ प्रयोक्तुमित्याधारया यदुपयोगि तदाह स्वर्तालानुभावकमिति (अभिनव भारती), ibid, p.302

97　"एक एव तु प्रकार: कलाविधिना निबध्यमानो राघवविजयमारीचवधादिकं रागकाव्यभेदमुद्द्रावयतीति ।यथोक्त (कोहलेन)

"लयांतरप्रयोगेण रागैश्चापि विवेचितम्। नानारसं सुनिर्वाह्य कथं काव्यमिति स्मृतम्।।

लयतश्चास्य गीत्याधारत्वेनाप्राधान्ये गीतेरेव प्राधान्यमिति न काव्यार्थविपर्यासवशेन रागभाषादिविपर्यासो नाट्य इव।

तथा हि राघवविजयस्य हि ठक्करागेणैव विचित्रवर्णीयत्वेऽपि निर्वाह:।मारीचवधस्य ककुभग्रामरागेणैव ।अतएव रागकाव्यानीत्युच्यंत एतानि।रागो गीत्यात्मकत्वास्तव (क: स्व) रस्य तदाधारभूतं काव्यमिति ।" वही,पृष्ठ 184.

98　Radhavallabh Tripathi, Sanskrit Sahitya ka Abhinav Itihas, Viswavidyalaya Prakashan, Varanasi, First Edition 2001, p. 205

which is considered to be the earliest specimen of New Indo-Aryan vernacular literature, was composed in various meters; it also indicates the raga that is appropriate to each composition.[99] It is interesting to note that the famous thirteenth-century treatise on Indian music, *Sangītaratnākara*, categorises Caryāgīti in the group it calls *prakīrṇakaprabandhagīti*, in which songs are composed in meter with end-rhyme.[100] The question arises as to whether it was *suras* (tunes) or rather words that comprised the more central element in this kind of composition, or is it possible to take both into account simultaneously? Studying early eastern New-Indo-Aryan versification, Nilratan Sen opines that "... from the context of the songs it [becomes clear] that the text of the song was no less important...than the tune. So, obviously, the composers were inclined to maintain a recital verse-meter, side by side with the raga-tune. Versification and musical notes therefore often overlapped."[101]

Subsequently this style came down to Hindi poetry, as Ganapatichandra Gupta proclaims, but only after bifurcating into two streams. In one stream Sanskrit poets like Kshemendra and Jayadeva adopted and developed it after being influenced by Apabhramsha poets. This tradition was adopted from Jayadeva by Maithili poets like Vidyapati, and that in turn

---

99 Out of 47 songs in Caryagitikosa 36 are composed in Padakulaka, 11 in Doha, Chaupai and others chhand and the following ragas are indicated in the text :Patamanjari, Gabadi, Malasi, Malasi Gabuda, Aru, Gujari, Kahnugunjari, Debakri Desakh, Bharabi, Kamoda, Dhanasi, Ramakri, Gauda Badadi,Sibari,Baladdi,Mallari,Bangala.see,Caryagitikosa (ed.) Nilratansen,Indian Institute of Advanced Study, Simla, First Edition,1977

100 Sarangadeva, Sangitaratnakar, Tr.R.K.Shringy and Premlata Sharma, Munshiram Manoharlal, New Delhi,1991,Sloka 292-294

101 Nilratan Sen, Early Eastern NIA Versification, Indian Institute of Advanced Study, Simla, First Edition, 1973, p.4.

was later popularised by Krishnaite poets. In the other stream the lyric style of siddhas was developed by the Nāthpanthī yogis and Maharashtrian *sants*, creating a tradition that later came down to the Hindi *sant* poets.[102] Thus a tradition was established in north India where meter or music became a part of an overall communication strategy; and in this regard there was no difference between *saguna* and *nirguna*, between *krishnabhakta* and *rāmabhakta*, or between *prem-margī* and *gyān-mārgī*.

We can see the importance of musical systems of classification in the case of the Ādigranth. This great book classifies its contents on the basis of various ragas. After an initial three *vānīs* the remaining poems, comprising the great bulk of the collection, are arranged in thirty-one ragas.[103] The same is the case with Sindhi poetry, where, in the words of Ali S.Asani,

The thematic relationship between musical mode and Sindhi mystical poetry is demonstrated explicitly in early manuscripts in which poems were arranged in chapters according to the *sur* in which they were intended to be sung. The first collection to be so arranged was that of Miyān Shāh'Ināt ('Ināyatullāh Rizwī), whose poems were grouped under nineteen *surs*. The great classical compendium of Sindhi mystical poetry, Shāh'Abdul Latīf's *Risālo*, is arranged into thirty chapters, each devoted to

---

102 Ganpati Chandra Gupta, Sahityik Nibandh, Lokbharti Prakashan, Allahabad, sixth edition, 1977, p. 364

103 The Adigranth is a compiled work of five centuries (12th to 17th) and its final editing was completed in 1604 but earlier manuscripts also indicate Ragas. see, Adigranth, Maheep Singh, Rajpal and Sons, Delhi, First Edition, 2009, p.28-29

a *sur*, and most of these are associated with either a specific folktale or a certain theme.[104]

As it was evident in the case of *Caryāgītikośa*, there were two ways of presenting poetry in the north Indian tradition—one way was reciting and the other was singing. Both these traditions were developed, it seems, in the process of acquiring better skills in communication. Recitation requires familiarity with meter (*chand*), whereas knowledge of raga is must for singing. It is no coincidence that before elaborating various ways of poetry recitation in his *Kāvyamīmāṃsā*, Rajashekhara (10th century) establishes the importance of recitation itself in no uncertain terms: "Experts in poetry writing may somehow compose poems, but only the accomplished can recite poetry."[105] *Prabandhas* or larger works were meant for recitation, so a *prabandha* like the *Rāmcaritmānas* mentions the name of its *chands,* whereas smaller works or *muktakas* were for singing. No wonder most of the *padas* of Kabir, Mira or Surdas, or of Tulsi's *Vinaya Patrikā* and *Gītāvalī,* indicate the names of the ragas to which they were to be sung.[106] But both the traditions were one in aiming at *rasa* as the fruition of the performance process overall.

---

104 Ali S. Asani, At the crossroads of Indic and Iranian Civilizations: Sindhi Literary Cultures in Sheldon Pollock (ed.), Literary Cultures in History, University of California Press, Berkley and Los Angeles, California, 2003, p.633

105 करोति काव्यं प्रायेण संस्कृतात्मा यथा तथा। पठितुं वेत्ति स परं यस्य सिद्धा सरस्वती।। Rajshekhar, Kavya Mimansa, Bihar Rashtrabhasha Parishad, Patna, Third Edition, 2000, p. 82

106 This is also worth-mentioning here that ritikalin poetry does not mention either raga's name or chhanda's name but Bhartendu tries it again in 19th century—he not only indicates ragas but chhanda's name also and sometimes both in the same text. In Chayavad both Sumitranandan Pant and SuryakantTripathy 'Nirala' thought necessary to delve over the relationship between Chand and Rasa in the poetry albeit from different angles.

Kshemendra (990–1065 C.E.) instructs poets that they should select the meters (*chand*) they use according to the subject being described and the *rasa* that is inherent in the poetry.[107] Bhanukavi also provides a table of favourable and unfavourable meters according to *rasas* and the subject matters being described. Buthe emphasizes that the system works better for Sanskrit than for Bhasha. Vernacular meters like *dohā, chaupaī, soraṭh, savaiyā*, etc., are suitable for all kinds of *rasa* and subject.[108]

The question of the relation between raga and *rasa* has been addressed since the time when the *Nāṭyaśāstra* was written. When Bharatamuni discusses "the occasions and *rasas* of the *dhruvās*," he says:

There are two kinds of occasions: One which relates to others, and one which relates to oneself.

The ApakṛṣṭaDhruvā should be sung in the Karuṇa Rasa on the following occasions: when captured, when obstacles are encountered, during a fall, illness, fainting or death.

A SthitaDhruvā (a Dhruvā with the VilambitaLaya) should be sung on these occasions: when in a desperate hurry, when dissimulating, when worried, when tired, when extremely depressed, when in despair.

When these emotions are being expressed in the Karuṇa Rasa, the Karuṇa emotions should be expressed in the DrutaLaya.

Grief on personally seeing someone dead or wounded should be acted in the Sthita (Vilambita) Dhruvā and the Karuṇa Rasa.

---

107 काव्ये रसानुसारेण वर्णनानुगुणेन च ।कुर्वीत सर्ववृत्तानां विनियोगं विभागवित् ॥7॥ Kshemendra, Suvrattilakam, Chaukhamba Sanskrit Series Office, Varanasi, First Edition, 1968, p. 109

108 Jagannath Prasad 'Bhanukavi', Chand Prabhakar, Sri Venkateswara Press Bombay, 1931

The Dhruvā should be sung in the Druta Laya on these occasions: on seeing unexpected calamities, when intensely happy, on seeing something astounding, when depressed, when pleased, in anger, on seeing heroic acts, when personally reporting the heroic, the furious and the terrible. The Dhruvā should be sung in the DrutaLaya on occasions of excitement.

The Prāsādikī Dhruvā should be sung in the Madhya Laya on these occasions: when pacifying another, when making a request, when remembering (various things), when making an exaggerated speech, in a first meeting, on seeing the unusual in love.

The Antarā Dhruvā should be sung continuously when there is physical distress, in anger and when wielding weapons.

The Dhruvā should not be sung when the character enters weeping or singing, or when there is a hasty action, or when giving a message, or if a mishap (falling, stumbling, etc.) or something surprising occurs when entering.

The Dhruvā-s should thus be used after taking into consideration the theme, the region, time, season, the characters and emotions.[109]

The relation of a raga to a mental state is a complex albeit intriguing subject. Acharya Brahaspati, in his pioneering work *Bhārat kā Sangīt Siddhānt,* proposes a clear-cut relationship between *sthayī-svara,*

---

109 Adya Rangacharya, Natyasastra, English Translation with Critical Notes, Munshram Manoharlal Publishers Pvt.Ltd.Fourth edition, 2003, pp.287–288;

Table 1   *rasa,* and *sthayī-bhāva*: [110] see, Table 1

Major Notes (Sthayee Swara)	Rasa	Major Emotions (Sthayee Bhava)
Shadaj (sa)	Valour (Veer), Splendid (Adbhut), Terror (Raudra)	Enthusiasm (Utsah,) Wonder (vismai), Anger (krodha)
Risabh (re)	do	do
Gandhar (ga)	Pathos (Karun)	Sorrow (shoka)
Madhyam (ma)	Erotic (Shringar), Humour (Hasya)	Love (Rati), Laughter (Haasa)
Pancham (pa)	do	do
Dhaivat (dha)	Disgust (Vibhatsa), Dread (Bhyanak)	Fear (Bhaya), Repulsion (Jugupsa)
Nishad (ni)	Pathos (Karuna)	Sorrow (shoka)

Picking up the same subject, Omkarnath Thakur, the great musician of twentieth-century India, once remarked that it is not merely the notes which produce a mood but also various other factors like graces, tempo, octave levels and so on. According to him those ragas moving in the upper octaves are never somber and dignified; they express faster-paced emotions such as anger,

---

110 Kailash Chandradev Brihaspati, Bharat ka Sangeet siddhant, Uttar Pradesh Hindi Sansthan, Lucknow, Second Edition, 1991, p.271

excitement and enthusiasm. Those with an emphasis on the *sa-ma* relation, by contrast, are peaceful and mature. Ragas of the *khamaj*group are erotic and lighter in vein. Those with *ri, dha,* and *ma* have pathos as their predominant tendency. Ragas with *ri, dha,* and *ma* show tiredness, lack of enthusiasm, etc.[111] Thus classical aesthetic criticism offers us an array of matters to be considered when we assess the relationship between poetry and music.

To test such notions in relation to the devotional poetry of early modern north India, let us consider the edition of his work net us a total of sixteen ragas. For the 201 *padas* of Mira in Parshuram Chaturvedi's edition an aggregate of seventy ragas are indicated. Tulsidas' *Gītāvalī* in the Gita Press edition consists of 330 *padas,* in which 22 ragas are mentioned, while the Gita Press edition of his *Vinaya Patrikā* offers 279 *padas,* for which 23 ragas are listed. As for Surdas, if you accept the *skandha* method of arranging poems in the *Sūrsāgar* and restrict our attention to only the first canto (*prathama skandha*), you come up with 343 *padas,* for which 28 ragas are indicated. These distributions can be seen in Tables 2 and 3.

---

111 Quoted in B.Chaitnaya Deva, The Music of India: A Scientific Study, Munshram Manoharlal
Publishers Pvt. Ltd. 1995. p.142

Table 2

Poets	Edition	Total no. of Padas	Total no. of Padas in which Ragas are indicated	No. of indicated Ragas
Kabir	Kabir Granthavali, Shyam Sundar Das, (ed) Lokbharti Prakashan, Allahabad 2nd edition 2011	403	403	16
Surdas	Sursagar Satik, Hardev Bahari, Rajendra Kumar, (ed.) Lokbharti Prakashan, Allahabad, Feb, 1991	343 (Pratham Skandh)	324	28
Meera	Meerabai ki Padavali, Parshuram Chaturvedi (ed.), Hindi Sahitya sammelan, Prayag, Allahabad, 19th edition, 1993	201	115	70
Tulsidas	Geetavali, Geeta Press, Gorakhpur, Fourteenth edition, Samvat 2041	330	143	22
	Vinay Patrika, Geeta Press, Gorakhpur, 52nd edition, Samvat 2057	279	46	23

If we take as our guide the editions mentioned in Table 2, then we see in Table 3 that in comparison to the other three poets Mira used the greatest variety of ragas, even though she composed the smallest number of *padas*. If we agree with the critics' general evaluation of Mira's limited life experience and the relative monotony that it produced in her poetry,[112] then it is quite understandable that she would have wanted to introduce variety into her oeuvre by means of the numerous ragas she employed. Contrary to this, Kabir is considered to be well informed about the world[113] and to be, like Narsimha, a witness to varied and sometimes almost impossible situations,[114] so it is no wonder that, in comparison to the other three poets, he has the least need to introduce variety into his poetry by means of a plethora of ragas. Can we draw a conclusion from this contrast, proposing that the choice of ragas that would be appropriate to their verse had different meanings for different poets?

I think we can. For someone like Mira, raga was a device; it seems to compensate for her limited experience and exposure. Since every raga has a distinct form that interprets or colours the sensibilities of a text in a distinct way, the varieties expressed in ragas turn out to indicate varieties in sensibilities. Poets like Kabir, Tulsi, or Surdas, however, draw no extra weight from or

---

112 Parashuram Chaturvedi (ed.), Mirabai's Padavali, Hindi Sahitya Sammelan, Prayag, Nineteenth Edition, 1993, pp. 31–32

113 Shyam sundar Das (ed.), Kabir Granthawali, Lokbharti Prakashan, Allahabad, Second Edition 2011, p. 37

114 Hajariprasad Dwivedi, Kabir, Rajkamal Prakashan, Delhi. 1994, p.144

19.Tulsidas, Vinaypatrika, Geeta Press, Gorakhpur, fifty-second edition 2000, p. 13 20. Hardev Bahri, Rajendra Kumar (ed.), Sursagar-Sateek first part, Lokbharti Prakashan, Allahabad, revised edition 1991, p. 1 21. Parasuram Chaturvedi, same, p.129

22. Shyamsundar Das, same, page 205

attention to a given raga in relation to their poetic compositions. They feel little need to expand their sensibilities. This argument can be substantiated by the number of ragas that we can discover to be specific to individual poets. In the case of Mira, we have fifty such ragas, whereas Surdas has six, and Kabir and Tulsi, three each, as documented in Tables 3 and 4.

Tables 4 and 5 present information that further amplifies our sense of the landscape of word and song in bhakti poetry. In Table 4 we have a representation of the ragas most commonly used by our four major poets, taken in the aggregate. Then in Table 5 we see the ragas individually preferred by the poets concerned. The ragas that they hold in common are *dhanāśrī,* āsāvarī, *sārang, rāmkelī, bilāval, malār, māru,* and *todī.*

Surveying the data presented in Tables 4 and 5, we have two options. Either we see the structure of a particular raga—what it "expresses" by its constituent notes—and then see how this accords with the contents of a particular poem, imagining each to be invariant in time; or we try to perceive a particular raga and its corresponding poem in a diachronic setting, judging that neither the raga's structure nor the poem's meaning is static. To acquire the additional data that would make this latter approach feasible is very difficult. It is almost impossible to ascertain the structure of a given raga as it would have been performed in the bhakti period. It is equally difficult to know how our four bhakti poets might have perceived such a raga at that point of time, a bit of information that would seem to be required to determine a given

Table 4

Poets	Five Most Preferred Raga-s in terms of its usage					No. of Ragas Common among All four poets	No. of Ragas specific to Individual Poets
Kabir	Gaudi (152)	Asavari (60)	Ramkali (49)	Sorathi (38)	Bhairav (37)	09	03
Surdas	Dhanashree (83)	Sarang (55)	Bilaval (35)	Kedar (26)	Kanhara (19)	09	06
Meera	Piloo (6)	Sarang (5)	Bihag (4)	Sorath (4)	Bilaval (3)	09	50
Tulsidas	Kedara (29)	Bilaval (16)	Kanhara (13)	Gauri (13)	Jaitshree (11)	09	03

Table 5

Common Raga-s	Kabir (1400–1520)	Surdas (1479–1582)	Meera (1498–1562)	Tulsidas (1532–1623)
Dhanashree	06	83	01	08
Asavari	60	09	01	10
Sarang	02	55	05	09
Sorath	38	12	05	14
Ramkali	49	11	01	07
Bilaval	12	35	03	16
Malar	02	10	01	06
Maru	03	07	01	06
Todi	02	03	01	09

poem's communicability with the raga in question.[115] From the early twentieth century onward, when gramophone companies started recording in India, we have enough data to show that singers hardly make a habit of following the ragas indicated on the page as they prepare to render the compositions of bhakti poets. How is this to be understood? Maybe the sensibilities expressed in the meaning of the poems has changed in the

---

115 Here we also take note of Winand M. Callewaert who looking for the original version of Kabir found 'musical' variants very important; he says: "It would appear that first the singers sang a particular song in a particular rag, then they grouped together the songs which were to be sung in the same rag.Consequently, a rag is like an identity card for the earliest period of oral transmission. The same song, however, could be sung to different raga-s in different manuscripts. The variation in classification is obviously not due to a scribe's intervention, but stems from the oral period itself when the songs were transmitted under different raga-s and appeared as such in the manuscripts." The Millennium Kabir Vani, Manohar, Delhi, First published 2000, p.103

course of time—or, alternatively, there have been changes in the interpretation of the ragas involved. Or perhaps both.

The situation is complex. We can see what is involved by considering the example of raga *bilāval. Bilāval* is a morning raga, intended to be sung between 6 and 9 a.m., preferably in the rainy season, and with a feeling of deep devotion and repose. *Bilāval* was a popular raga in the medieval period. No wonder, then, that over 170 hymns were composed to this raga by Guru Nanak, Guru Amar Das, Guru Ram Das, Guru Arjan and Guru Tegh Bahadur, as recorded in the Ādi *Granth*. It later became a basic *ṭhāṭh* (musical mode) in Hindustani classical music. *Bilāval* is considered by most authorities to be of the *sampūrṇa-sampūrṇa jāti.* Others, however, are of the opinion that it should be considered śadav-sampūrṇa due to the weakness of its *ga* in the ascent (ārohana) of the raga. In ascending, the following *svaras* appear: *sa re ga ma pa dha ni sa.* In descending, the following: *sa ni dha pa ma ga re sa.* Its *vādi* is *dha* and its *saṃvādi* is *ga.* The *calan* or *pakaḍ,* is: *ga re, ga ma dha pa, ma ga, ma re sa.* So there are some uncertainties in evaluating *bilāval* as we presently know it, but there are well accepted generalizations, as well.

Now what can we see if we consider four actual uses of *bilāval* on the part of our exemplary bhakti poets? Tulsi Das's *Vinaya Patrikā* begins with a hymn to lord Ganesha in this raga:

गाइए गनपति जग बन्दन। संकर-सुवन भवानी-नन्दन॥

सिद्धि-सदन, गज-बदन, द बिनायक।कृपा-सिन्धु, सुन्दर, सब-लायक॥

मोदक-प्रिय, मुद-मंगल-दाता। विद्या-बारिधि, बुधि-विधाता॥

मांगत तुलसीदास कर जोरे। बसहिं राम सिय मानस मोरे।[116]

---

116 Tulsidas, Vinaypatrika, Geeta Press, Gorakhpur, fifty-second edition 2000, p. 13

Surdas also begins his *mangalācaraṇ* in raga *bilāval*:

चरनकमलबन्दौ हरि राइ।जाकीकृपापंगु गिरि लंघैअन्धेकौसबकछुदरसाइ।।[117]

On one occasion Mira employs *bilāval* for a poem that starts thus:

आवो मनमोहनाजी मीठी थारो बोल।।टेक।।

बालपनां की प्रीत रमैयाजी, कदेनाहिं आयो थारो तोल।

दरसण विणमोहि जकणपरत है, चित्त मेरोडावांडोल।

मीरा कहै मैंभईबावरी, कही बजाउं ढोल।।100 ।।[118]

Finally, Kabir gives us a *pada* in raga *bilāval* that begins as follows:

बारबार हरिकागुणगावै, गुरगमि भेद सहर कापावै।टेक।।[119]

If we analyze these poems, we find a certain similarity in their contents as well as in their forms, and each of these seems well suited to the patterns of raga *bilāval* as they have been set out above. So far, then, we seem to be on solid footing. But in present time, if we take for example Tulsidas' first Ganesha hymn, so very popular across the musical genres, we find that hardly anybody sings it in raga *bilāval*. Three symptomatic examples can be cited: Ashwini Bhide's rendering of this poem in raga *bihāg*,[120] Pandit Rajan and Sajan Mishra's rendering in raga *kirvānī*,[121] and Ahmed Hussain and Muhammad Husain's

---

117 Hardev Bahri, Rajendra Kumar (ed.), Sursagar-Sateek, first part, Lokbharti Prakashan, Allahabad, revised edition 1991, p. 1 21.

118 Parasuram Chaturvedi, ibid p.129

119 Shyam sundar Das, ibid, page 205

120 http://www.youtube.com/watch?v=D01xA03C8yE

121 Bhaktimala: Ganesh, vol 1, Music Today, 1991

rendering in rag *mārvā.*[122] If we compare the characteristics of these ragas with those appropriate to raga *bilāval*, we get the following spread (**Table 6**):

Raga	Nature	Jati	Singing time
Bilawal	devotional	Sampurna - Sampurna	Morning
Bihag	serious	Audav-sampoorna	Late night
Kirwani	melancholic	Sampurna - Sampurna	Mid-night
Marwa	contemplative	Shadav-Shadav	Sun set

As the table shows, these four ragas are so different in nature that their suitability for the above mentioned poem can only be interpreted as an act of individual perception on the part of the performer. Ragas have different possible meanings just as poems do; there are multiple possibilities in each case. Ragas not only differ from one another as a class, they also vary according to individual usage. When it comes to an act of poetic communication between words and music, then, it is not just a question of which raga will best suit a given poem, but which is best suited to communicate its meaning in a given moment. Or, to work backwards, which poem is best suited to give "voice" to a given raga?

In the end, then, we can only return to the conundrum with which we began: Is it poetry in ragas or ragas in poetry? It sees it must indeed be both.

---

122 Shradha, T-series, 1995

6

BINDADIN MAHARAJ AND THE EVOLUTION OF KATHAK*

The emergence of Kathak as a modern dance form is a recent phenomenon though its evolution can be traced in antiquity, right from the Mohenjo-Daro to Vedic times to Ramayana-Mahabharata age to Bhakti period[123]; but as Kathak danseuse Sobhana Narayan puts it, *"it was only in late 18th century that the personal interest of a select few, particularly Nawab Asaf-ud-daula and later Nawab Wajid Ali Shah of Oudh who had their capital at Lucknow, saw Kathak emerging from the confines of the closet of Hindu temples and make its entry into the Muslim court, without*

---

123 But some scholars argue that it was imported from Persia: For instance, Mandakranta Bose cites a Mughal Period treatise the Nartananirnaya, in which a style was described that, "it says was practised by Persian dancers; from its description we can identify this style as the present day Kathak, and from other historic sources we know that this style was indeed imported to India by Persian court dancers in the Mughal era." see, Mandakranta Bose, Movement and Mimesis: The Idea of Dance in the Sanskritic Tradition, Springer & Kluwer AcademicPublishers, 1991, p.259

* This paper was Presented online in the 14th International Conference on Early Modern Literatures of North India at Osaka University, Japan on 19th July 2022

diluting its original pristine flavour.it was the fame of Thakur Prasad, a Kathak, whose family had originally been attached to a small temple in the tehsil of Hadia (region near Allahabad) that was instrumental in seeing him become a guru to Nawab Wajid Ali Shah ..."[124] That was the time when regional power centres were evolving after the disintegration of central Mughal empire. Abdul Halim Sharar (1860–1926) chronicles in *Guzista Lucknow* the dance scenario under the reign of Nawab Wajid Ali Shah in following words: *"There are two groups of male dancers in Lucknow: the Hindu Kathaks and rahas dancers, and the Kashmiri Muslim bhands. The real dancers are Kathaks...*

"There have always been accomplished Hindu Kathaks in Lucknow. At the time of Shuja ud Daula and Asaf-ud-Daula, Khushi Maharaj was a very expert dancer, In the days of Nawab Sadat Ali Khan, Ghazi ud Din Haider and Nasir-ud Din Haider, Hallal Ji, Prakash Ji, and Dayalu Ji were celebrated dancers from the time of Muhammad Ali shah until Wajid Ali Shah's reign, Durga Prasad and Thakur Prasad, sons of Prakash Ji, were famous. It is said that Durga Prasad taught Wajid Ali Shah to dance. Later the two sons of Durga Prasad, Kalka and Bindadin became renowned and nearly everyone acknowledged that no one in the whole of India could rival either of them at dancing. The older experts achieved fame because of some particular aspect of the art but these two brothers, especially Bindadin, were masters of every aspects...

"His dancing to gat, his portrayal of delicate technical aspects of tora and tukra, the superb control with which he makes as many bells on his ankles as he likes resound, is individual to him and

---

124 Shovona Narayan, Kathak, A Shubhi Publication Enterprise, First economy edition, 2012, pp.88–89

beyond all compare. He gives to every steps and gesture a hundred fascinations and embodies in them a variety of subtle perceptions. His deft movements and originality are such that the onlooker, unless well-versed in the art, is unable to follow them.

"Binda Din used to perform batana depiction through bodily movements and Kalka use to give a verbal interpretation. From this commentary people were able to realise how perfect Binda Din was in displaying his art. When dancing, his feet touched the ground so lightly that he used to dance sometimes on the edges of swords and come to no harm." [125] Here what is described about the art of Bindadin Maharaj (1830–1918) says something about how the evolution in Kathak at that point of time was taking place.

Gat, Tora, Tukra, Ghungharoo, Tatkar to Bhavabhivyanjana or Bhav-batana is a process similar to the journey of *Nritt to Nritya.*In Natyashastra nrtta (नृत्त), is a non-representational art that is 'devoid of either rasa or bhava and is based on sheer physical gestures and movements supported by tempo (or laya and tala), while natya (नाट्य) and nritya (नृत्य) convey rasa and bhava respectively.'[126] Nandikesvara in *Abhinaya Darpana* also defines Nritt as: भावभिनयाहींन नृतमित्यभिधीयते means Nrtta is that form of dance which is void of flavour (rasa) and mood (bhava)[127] and Dhananjay in Dasroopak says नृत्तं ताललयाश्रम *Nrittm talalayashram*[128] that means Tala and laya are the basic concepts of nritta. Over the years Nritta was incorporated in

---

125 Abdul Halim Sharaar, Lucknow The Last Phase of the Oriental Culture in the Lucknow Omnibus, OUP, New Delhi, India, 2001, p.142

126 K. M. Varma, Natya, Nritta and Nritya, Orient Longmans, Calcutta, First Published, 1957, p.1

127 Anand Coomaraswamy, The Mirror of Gesture, Munshiram Manoharlal, Delhi, fourth edition 1987, p.14

128 धनञ्जय, दशरूपकम, (सं)श्रीनिवास शास्त्री, साहित्य भण्डार, मेरठ, 1994, पृष्ठ 10

the first section of a dance performance that involves bodily movements and consists of chari, rechika, Angaharas, Karanas, Bhramaris, Nrittahastas etc. and when bhavabhinaya was incorporated into it became more compounded and complex. Working on the question why later texts on dance deviated from the earlier propositions, Mandakranta Bose concludes, *"This shift in the understanding of dancing shows that the separate techniques of nrtta and abhinaya, or acting, came to be regarded as complementing one another within the framework of nritya. This development suggests that as dance evolved, it was nritya that developed the more vigorously.*[129] This conclusion was drawn on the basis of Sanskrit theoretical work on dance but if we compare what Kutuban provided us the details of a dance-performance in Mrigavati (1503) with the above description of Bindadin's performance, it sounds true. Kutuban describes a dance performance in Mrigavati 'court in following words:

फुनि पुतरी कछनी कै आई। मान बहुत लावहिं बहु भाई।।

केवल बदन मृगनैनी सुहाई। वरें लंक जानु उन्ह लाई।।

हिया सुभर जनु कुंद सँवारी। कदलि खंभ पेड़ न संभारि।।

चम्पा बरन सुहानी तरूनी, जो देखत सो मोह।

बेगर बेगर भाँ तिंह कै, कै आई छोह।।

कछनी दखिन क चीर कै गहीं। चंदर चोलि उर लेइ रहीं।।

अभरन समै कपूर क कीन्हां। घाँघरि बाँधि आइ पग दीन्हा।।

चीहुर गूँद बेनी उरबाई। चन्दन रूख पर बिसहर छाई।।

देखत मोहि सभा सब रही। काम चेष्टा तन मन गही।।

कै जुहार उन्ह आयसु लीन्हा। कुँवर नाँच कँह आयसु दीन्हा।।

---

129 Mandakranta Bose, ibid, p.256

गायन गावहिं काढि सुधांग, नाच होई तिह लाग।

माँथा धौरा झूमरा परिबंध यह र गीत वै राग।।

सरब नील रूपक चंद औ चाली।देसी जित पँवर इकताली।।

अठतालो पटताली नाचीं। ताल देन्हि जानहु घर ताचीं।।

फुनि नाचइ धर पला सँचारा। नाचहिं गीत होइ झनकारा।।

सीस नियर कूदहिं मँह मोतीं। दहा दिहिंह चक्र भँवहि उरधूती।।

सरो अकाँच खरगै धारा। मान लेहिं पर ताल निपारा।।

नाचै ताल सवै उन्ह कँटमारग जहाँ लहि राग।

सुरपति सुरहिं साथ लै, कौतुक अवसर देखै लाग।[130]

Now Aditya bahl translated it in these following words:

Then the dancers came in, dressed in short saris.

They put on many airs and graces.

They had lotus faces and lovely doe eyes.

Their waists seemed to be taken from wasps.

Their breasts were white as jasmine blossoms.

Their legs were smooth as plantain trees, and as full.

Magnolia-colored, those lovely young women enchanted all who saw them.

Many different moods they had, and many ways of demonstrating

love.

---

130 कुतुबन, मिरगावती, (सं.)परमेश्वरी लाल गुप्त, विश्वविद्यालय प्रकाशन, वाराणसी, प्रथम संस्करण, 1967, पृष्ठ 288–290

Their tight, short saris were from the southland.

They had applied their blouses to their breasts

like sandal paste. Their ornaments were camphor scented.

They tied on their ankle-bells and began their steps.

They had braided their hair and let it hang

Like black cobras covering sandalwood trees.

The whole assembly saw them and was entranced.

Passionate desire seized their minds and bodies.

The dancers salaamed the prince, sought his permission.

The prince ordered them to begin the performance.

The singers sang intensely, and they were accompanied by spirited dances.

The manthā, the dhruvā, the ring-dance, and the paribandha— these were the songs, those the melodies.

They danced to all the rhythmic cycles:

the nīla, the rūpaka, and the candacālī,

the desī, the jati, the tevarī, the eka-tālī,

the asta-tāla, and the pata-tālī.

They followed the beat, their bodies taut,

then began to dance the dhruva-pada.

They sang songs and the music rang out.

They carried water-pots and strung pearls

with their mouths, those dancing girls,

Whirling saris around their thighs, wheel-like.

They danced with bowls, on glass, and on sword's edge,

Proudly beating out the various rhythms.

They danced to all the different rhythms, usages, songs, and melodies that existed.[131]

It was the beginning of 16th century and it is not very clear from the description that what dancers are performing is nritta or nritya? It seems not only the vocabulary of music, rhythm and dance styles were different at that point of time but the very performance costumes were different. If we see some illustrated manuscripts like Kalpasutra of 15th century we do find dancers wearing tight south-Indian sarees up to their knees with tight blouses (see, Appendix B), but from 16th century onwards they are mostly wearing ghagra-choli or long skirt and blouses. (see, Appendix C) Morever, What is described here about their dancing the Sudhanga, (?) Manthā, the Dhaura (dhruvā?), the Jhumara (Bhramari?), Paribandha (Prabandha, that is a kind of Geet, as *Sangeetratnakar* defines?), on various rhythmic cycles:the Sarab nil (sarpnīla), the rūpaka, and the canda-o-cālī (?), the desī, the jati, the tevarī (?), the eka-tālī, the attha-tāla, and the pata-tālī— with bowls, on glass, and on sword's edge, carrying water-pots and strung pearls with their mouths, Whirling saris around their thighs like wheel are little puzzling. It appears now that either some of these practices and vocabulary in Kathak of that time are not in practice or changed to such an extent that

---

131   Aditya Behl and Wendy Doniger (Tr. And ed.) The Magic Doe: Qutban Suhravardi's Mirigavati, Oxford University Press, USA, 2012, p.133

now it is difficult to even decipher it. We don't know exactly what does Sarba nil (sarpanil?) Sudhanga, (?) Manthā, the Dhaura (dhruvā?) mean; is it a kind of dance -style or musical forms or compositions? whether it is part of Nritt or Nritya? Madhu Trivedi mentions that *according to the author of Ghunyat al-munya, a fourteenth century Persian musical treatise, sarp-nil was like chaturang and its four segments were performed in different rags, tals and languages. This composition apparently went out of vogue as we do not find its mention in the medieval musical literature. Chaturang, however, persisted even in the nineteenth century and we find it performed by the dancers of Awadh court.*[132] It seems probable that the four segment of sarpnil or chaturang must be envisioned to incorporate all the related resources available at that point of time; after all this is how evolution takes place. In this regard the view of Kapila Vatsyayan is worth mentioning, she writes: *Kathak, the abhinaya portions have evolved out of many traditions known to central India. The rasdharis of Mathura and Vrindavan, the dancers of Gujarat and dance kirtans of Bihar and of the Maithili region are the precursors of the literary content of the Kathak dance... To the accompaniment of the song the dancer presents meaning through gesture, while it is not conclusively proven that Kathak as evolved in the court of Wajid Ali Shah deliberately discarded this religious content. In the practice until quite recently, the literary lyric had come to have secondary place.*[133]

The change in not only in abhinaya part of the dance performance but nritta too was, it seems the result of various

---

132 Madhu Trivedi, The Emergence of the Hindustani Tradition, Three Essays Collective, Gurgaon, First Edition 2012, pp.166–167

133 Kapila Vatsyayan, Indian Classical Dance, Publication Division, Delhi 2nd Reprint, 1997, pp.93–94

factors gathering towards two different and opposing pulls to Kathak, namely the raslila and thumri.[134] No wonder some art critic notices some dichotomies in the dance repertoire of Kathak; Margret Walker writes: *Characteristic Kathak dance vocabulary includes rhythmic footwork, which is often improvised and enhanced by ankle bells called ghunguru, and dizzying sequences of spins called chakkars. This energetic side is contrasted by flowing, sensual gestures used predominantly in expressive or narrative dances and contained for the most part in the arms, hands, and upper body. Kathak dancers' gestures and facial expressions are subtle and contrast with the more exaggerated, theatrical movements of other Indian dances. In what is considered its most traditional form, this distinctive vocabulary (energetic and sensual) finds expression through a performance practice consisting of a solo presentation of a series of short dance pieces that unfold over a gradually increasing tempo. The individual items or "numbers" range from the aforementioned expressive or narrative sections illustrating poetry or telling stories from Hindu mythology to complex composed rhythmic pieces closely related to North Indian drumming. Kathak*

---

134 "There is no sufficient historical evidence to determine a link of artistic relationship between the raslila dancing and the Kathak style of dance; and it is all the more difficult to say which style has borrowed from which. However there are some basic facts which prove and show many points of resemblance between the two styles of dancing. In the portrayal of emotions and situations, and in the general mode of storytelling by a vivid pantomimic gesture language, the two styles have a common character. Apart from the gesture, in the movements, turns, pauses and groupings of the characters in raslila during the dance and pantomime for depiction of the episodes, we find resemblances. ...some of the main 'gats'— the 'murali gat' and the 'panghat gat'—are common to both. Similarly, some of the 'kavitta-bols' and 'naatwari bols' are also common. 'Ta thei thei tat', the root-words (bij-akshar) of Kathak dance have been referred to by the Vaishnava poets in their kirtan songs." see, Raslila-A operatic Drama, S.Awasthi, in Mulk Raj Anand (ed.), Marg, volume XII, Number 4, September 1959, p.55

dance repertoire thus seems to comprise a number of dichotomies – rhythmic versus narrative, energetic versus flowing, devotional versus secular, and improvised versus pre-composed – that are witness to its syncretic development.[135]

If this formulation is true than other than Bindadin Maharaj, no other exponent of Kathak is more suitable for its example as he is the one who has negotiated these *dichotomies* in most creative way. Mohan Khakar observed, *Bindadin was a devout person. Hence the dance form that came into existence at this time, attempted a compromise between the two ideals: it became secular in character but it did not divorce itself from the Krishna-Radha theme or to put it another way, it continued to present the Krishna-Radha episodes but with a sensuous flavour.*[136] Art critic generally understood this *compromise* as reflection of the demand of changed environment —the shift from temple to court or from natwari to darbari nritya —that has made this compromise or adjustment, inevitable.[137] Perhaps this is the answer why Bindadin Maharaj composed so many bandishes when there was no dearth of it, even in his own family, his own grandfather's book *Pothi Prakas* was comprising so many things including 360 *gats*, of which, it is said that Wajid Ali Shah incorporated 16 in his book *Saut ul- Mubarak.* It may be inferred that rest of the gats were considered not suitable for the courtly

---

135 Margaret Walker, Revival and Reinvention in India's Kathak dance, Music Cultures 37, pp.173–174

136 Mohan Khakar, Schools of Kathak: Lucknow Gharana, Marg, ibid, p.11

137 There is an episode described in the commentary of Bhaktamal by Priyadas (1712) where a Hindu Kathak dancer named Narayandas was asked to perform in front of a Muslim ruler and how cleverly he placed his tulsimala and danced in front of it. See, Sunil Kothari, Lucknow Gharana in Rashmi Vajpayee (ed.), Kathak Prasang, Rajkamal Prakashan, Delhi, second edition, p.82

culture and when a devout person like Bindadin has to survive and establish himself and his school in such an environment he has to adjust and innovate. His innovations were as much the product of his subjective creativity as much the byproduct of these outer pressures. Bindadin and Kalka Prasad changed the very structure of Kathak. It is no exaggeration that what we see today in Kathak is the codification of 19th century and that is mostly done by Kalka-Bindadin duo, as Madhu Trivedi rightly pointed out that, *"Almost all the characteristics of the Kathak dance took shape at this time, such as amad, that-bandi, gat nikas, gat-bhava, and bhav-nikas.Depiction of the compositions like tatkar ke tukre, natwari ke tukre, and layakari also assumed great importance. Bindadin imparted vitality and variety to this dance form. He improved and elaborated the gat and endowed it with gracefulness. A gestural language was also evolved wherein the body as a whole was visualized as the prime medium of expression; a set of decorative gestures were introduced which became an integral part of the gats. He was the foremost, if not the first, to choreograph dance gat bandhana in Kathak. He could dance in all the taals and musical forms: dhrupad, Thumri, Dadara, Ghazal, and Bhajan. Thumri was his special forte which he taught to Gauhar Jan and Zohra Bai, the eminent courtesans of the period. He developed the ang of Thumri in Kathak and it became extremely popular among the courtesans of Lucknow and Banaras. Bindadin is also credited with creating the expressional form of Kathak. He also enhanced the dramatic content, known as natyang."*[138] When the whole emphasis shifted from Nritta to abhinaya and *bhavabhivyanjana*, the role of shabda or

---

138 Madhu Trivedi, The Emergence of the Hindustani Tradition, Three Essays Collective, Gurgaon, First Edition 2012, pp.177–179

literature that is part of natyang becomes crucial, no wonder Bindadin Maharaj wrote so many songs and composed it with such a subtle fineness that later became hallmark of the Lucknow gharana. It is said that he composed almost five thousand songs (bandishes) on different musical styles such as Thumri, Bhajan, Dadra, Sadra, Holi, Tarana, kheyal, Tappa, Pada, Jhoola etc., but unfortunately very few songs have survived.

Genre	Raag	Theme	Taal
Thumri (18)			
Sadara (1)	Sorath	Nayika-bhed Mugadha or Madhya nayika	Jhaptal
Dadara (4)	Gara, Chayanat	Nayika bhed Pragalbha nayika, Mugdha nayika, Madhya nayika,	Dadara, ektaal,
Hori (3)	Gara, Mishra Khamaj, Desh	Virhotkanthita nayika	Chanchar, Addha
Jhoola (1)	Desh		Roopak
Bhajan (3)	Sindura kafi, Mishra Gara, Vadahans		Dadara, Roopak

Birju Maharaj's Collection **Rasgunjan**

These songs were later collected and published by Nirmala Joshi and Birju Maharaj. Firstly Nirmala Joshi has presented six of his bandishes with English translation in Kathak special number of Marg in 1959[139] and later adding 13 more in the journal of Sangeet Natak Akademi.[140] Birju Maharaj also compiled thirty songs of Bindadin Maharaj (his grandfather's elder brother) in a book called *Ras Gunjan (1994)*.

Out of thirty songs of *Ras Gunjan*, eighteens are Thumri and if we compare with the list of Nirmala Joshi's collection, out of nineteen (19) seven (7) are the thumris in which three (3) are the common thumris in both the list and total number of common compositions are eight that means we have total 41 (30+19-7) compositions of Bindadin Maharaj. These songs primarily based on popular early-modern Braj themes of Hindi literature mainly Krishna-leela and Nayikabhed, though these two themes were quite dominant since Gita-Govind of Jayadeva in all art-forms of India. No wonder, Captain Augustus Willard observed in the early nineteenth century that, "if the songs of Hindoostan were classed by subjects, perhaps that recites the amorous of christnu (Krishna) would be the most voluminous." It is also true that the popularity of this theme rests in its ability to adapt different role for different purpose, if it is performed in a temple its meaning is completely different then what it conveys in a court settings; in other words context determines the meaning so a Krishna Bhakta like Bindadin Maharaj performs natwari nritya in a court it becomes different thing for a performing

---

139 Some songs of Bindadin Maharaj in Mulk Raj Anand, Marg, volume XII, Number 4, September 1959, p.62

140 Compositions of Bindadin Maharaj, Sangeet Natak Akademi bulletin, April 1960 https://www.indianculture.gov.in/compostitions-maharaj-bindadin

Genre	Raag	Taal	Theme
Thumri (7)	Hameer	Teen taal,	Krishna-Leela with gopikayen; Chhed-chhaad, Nayika-bhed
Dadara (4)	Gara, Chayanat	Dadara, Ektaal,	Nayika bhed Pragalbha nayika, Mugdha nayika, Madhya nayika,
Bhajan (3)	Sindura kafi, Mishra Gara, Vadahans	Dadara, Roopak	Birth of Krishna, Ram gun, dukh haran ram Krishna
Hori (4)		Chanchar, Kaharwa	Virhotkanthita nayika
Jhoola (1)	Desh	Roopak	Jhoolat Radhe Naval Kishore

Nirmala Joshi's Collection

artist and quite different for his patron and his courtiers. Let us imagine Bindadin Maharaj is performing a Thumri in the court of Wajid Ali Shah, the bandish is:

कान्ह देखो ठाढ़े है ब्रज की ओर
कैसे के जाऊं पनिया भरन मोरी आली
मोके सरकी चुनरिया छोर।
नित –नित छेड़ करत हम से, यही डर लागे
जो अपने बस कर मोहे पैये
फिर बिंदा श्याम बनेंगी पति मोरा।

Kanha stands athwart the path to braj!

How shall I go to fetch water, my friend?

He pulls my veil from my head.

Everyday does he sat on me!

I am afraid.

Says Binda,

"he hopes, to draw me to him

And become my husband!" (Tr. Nirmala Joshi)[141]

Now it is possible when dancer expressing nayika's feelings towards nayak in a very sensuous way during bol-banav that, it may happen that the audience achieves *Sadharanikaran* (impersonalisation) and having empathy with the heroine but if dancer has an image to express of Radha- having devotional or spiritual complain towards lord Krishna on a metaphysical plane ; what will happen to those audience who are happened to born and brought up in different cultural milieu —in other words when performer and audience are placed in two different contexts, it might lead to a situation where what becomes *rasodrek* (upsurge of Ras) for the dancer turns *rasabhas* (mere semblance of Ras) for the audience or vice versa. It is difficult to say with certainty that whether Pundit Bindadin Maharaj as a composer and dancer used Krishna theme for its capabilities to express his devotion to Krishna or a device to display his dance skill in front of his patrons and connoisseurs? In other words whether he chose a subject that was quite suitable for his performance or was it a kind of strategy for achieving the

---

141 Compositions of Bindadin Maharaj, ibid

both targets simultaneously? In similar situation Early-modern Braj Poet Bhikharidas (active in c.1725–1760) had a confession to make as he proclaims: आगे के सुकवि रीझिहैं तौ कविताई न तौ,/राधिका–कन्हाई सुमिरन को बहानो है।[142] (*If future poets like it then it is poetry / otherwise it is pretext to remember radhika-kanhai.)*" Undoubtedly future dancers liked Bindadin's performances irrespective of the fact that whether for him it was a pretext for remembering Radha-kanhai or not!

___

142 भिखारी दास, काव्य निर्णय, (सं) जवाहरलाल चतुर्वेदी, कल्याण दास एंड ब्रदर्स, वाराणसी, प्रथम संस्करण, 1956, पृष्ठ 3

7

GANDHI & ART*

"...there are so many superstitions rife about me that it has now become almost impossible for me to overtake those who have been spreading them. As a result, my friends' only reaction is almost invariably a smile when I claim I am an artist myself."[143]

What Gandhi said to Dilip Kumar Roy in above quotation is still prevalent. The reaction as smile has not changed as yet since we hardly discuss Gandhi in relation to Art (forget about talking Gandhi as an Artist!) though it is possible to probe it in so many ways—for example we can think about Gandhian Aesthetics— what Gandhi thought about Beauty and Art, what was his idea about literature, painting, music etc.; we can also analyze those works of films, plays, painting, music, sculpture, literature where Gandhi and Gandhism is the subject; It is also

---

143 Dilip Kumar Roy, Among the Great, Jaico Publishing House, Bombay, 1950, pp.65–66.

* This is an expanded version of a paper presented in the National seminar on Exclusion/Inclusion and Gandhian Strategies at Institute of Gandhian Thought and Peace Studies, University of Allahabad on 6th September 2008.

worth focusing Gandhi as litterateur and as a translator as his writing runs through hundreds of volumes in Gujarati and English.

Gandhian Aesthetics: The Aesthetics of *Satyagraha*

Truth is Beauty

In *Young India* dated 23.03.1921, Gandhi wrote Satyagraha is literally holding on to Truth and it means, therefore, Truth-force. Truth is soul or spirit. It is, therefore, known as soul force.[144] In some other place he proclaimed that "I see and find beauty in Truth or through Truth. All truth, not merely true ideas, but truthful faces, truthful pictures, or songs, are highly beautiful.... Truth may manifest itself in forms which may not be outwardly beautiful at all. Socrates, we are told, was the most truthful man of his time and yet his features are said to have been the ugliest in Greece. To my mind, he was beautiful because all his life was a striving after Truth, and you may remember that his outward form did not prevent Phidias from appreciating the beauty of Truth in him, though as an artist he was accustomed to see Beauty in outward forms also."[145] Here Gandhi stresses the dichotomy of *content* and *form* and takes side of the content and later he equates form with immorality:

"Take Oscar Wilde. I can speak of him, as I was in England at the time he was being much discussed and talked about...Wilde

---

144 Shriman Narayan (ed.), The Selected Works Of Mahatma Gandhi, vol. six, Navajivan Publishing House, Ahmedabad, Third Reprint Popular Edition, 1995, pp.180–81.(Young India, 23.03.1921)

145 Ibid, p288. (Young India, 13.11.1924)

saw the highest Art simply in outward forms and, therefore, succeeded in beautifying immorality."[146] The natural corollary of beautifying immorality is the formula: *Art for Art's sake* and Gandhi vehemently opposes it: "People who claim to pursue 'art for art's sake' are unable to make good their claim...art can only be a means to the end which we must all of us achieve."[147]On Gandhi's statement that *Truth is God*, Romain Rolland commented that "it appears to me that it lacks one important attribute of God: joy. For—and on this I insist–I recognize no God without joy"; Gandhi replied that he did not distinguish between art and truth. "I am against the formula, *Art for Art's sake*. For me, all art must be based on the truth. I reject beautiful things if, instead of expressing truth, they express untruth...To achieve truth in art I do not expect exact reproductions of external things. Only living things bring living joy to the soul and must elevate the soul."[148] Here, it seems that Gandhi was aware of the Imitation Theory of Plato and Aristotle and certainly he was in favour of Aristotle who, unlike Plato conceptualized imitation as *feigning* that, which is beyond the literal verisimilitude.[149] He was also deeply conscious of the fact what he proclaimed elsewhere that "Truth and untruth often co-exist; good and evil are often found together. In an artist also, not seldom the right perception of things and the wrong co-exist. Truly beautiful creations come when right perception is at work. If these moments are rare in life, they are also rare in Art."[150] This is a rare insight from a

---

146 Ibid, p287

147 Ibid

148 Quoted in Luis Fischer, The Life of Mahatma Gandhi, Indus (Harper Collins), New Delhi, Second Impression1993, p368.

149 See, Aristotle, Poetics, (Tr. Malcom Heath), Penguin Books, 1996.

150 Shriman Narayan, Ibid, p.289. (Young India, 13.11.1924)

satyagrahi, for whom life and art were not two distinct entities but one as he said once "For to me the greatest artist is surely he who lives the finest life."[151] It reminds us the great saying of Greek theoretician Longinus that great writing is the echo of a noble mind.[152] Certainly this is against the modernist theorem of impersonality where life and art is not considered one but Gandhi emphatically argues that "we have somehow accustomed ourselves to the belief that art is independent of the purity of private life. I can say with all the experience at my command that nothing could be more untrue. As I am nearing the end of my earthly life, I can say that purity of life is the highest and truest art. The art of producing good music from a cultivated voice can be achieved by many, but the art of producing that music from the harmony of a pure life is achieved very rarely."[153] In short, this is what *Sachchidanand* means. Gandhi explained this term to Romain Rolland by saying "Sat" meaning "truth", "chit" "that which lives" and "true knowledge"(i.e. not a knowledge void of true perception), and "Ananda" " ineffable joy". In this conception truth is inseparable from joy."[154]

USEFUL IS BEAUTIFUL

What is Useful is beautiful: Gandhi once remarked that "why can't you see the beauty of colour in vegetables?"[155] And again in other place he concluded that "Beauty divorced from utility

---

151 Ibid, p300

152 Longinus, On the sublime, (Tr.William Rhys Roberts), Garland, 1987.

153 Shriman Narayan, Ibid, p291.(Harijan, 19.02.1938)

154 Romain Rolland and Gandhi Correspondence, Publication Division, Delhi, Restored Edition 2017, p.209

155 Shriman Narayan, ibid, p292. (Harijan, 7-4-1946)

is inconceivable"[156]. For him utility in art means leading a man "one step forward on the path of morality and gives him elevated views."[157]

ART AS NATURE

Generally Art is discussed either with the reference of Nature or Culture. Nature is given whereas Culture is constructed. If we see Art as Nature; we tend to evaluate it as a natural object whereas Art as Culture expects to be treated as an artifact. Gandhi mostly perceives Art as Nature that's the reason he makes parallel between the two: "To me art, in order to be truly great, must, like the beauty of Nature, be universal in its appeal....It must be simple in its presentation and direct in its expression like the language of Nature."[158] No wonder when he was asked why he is so much against specialization he posed a counter question, "why don't you look the plain fact in the face that Nature, which must be the last inspiration of all real arts, never stints? She never specializes in a way so that only the cultured few may enjoy her bounties leaving the vast majority out in the cold."[159] In other place he asks," could one conceive of any painting comparable in inspiration to that of the star-studded sky, the majestic sea, the noble mountains? Is there a painter's colour comparable to the vermillion of an emergent dawn or the gold of a parting day? No, my friend, I need no inspiration other than Nature's. She has never failed me yet: she mystifies me, bewilders me, sends me into ecstasies. What need have I for the childish colour-schemes

---

156 Shriman Narayan, Ibid, pp.224-25 (The Diary of Mahadev Desai-1:1953)

157 ibid.

158 Ibid p299 (Among the Great, p.61–67)

159 Ibid p302 (ibid, pp.78–82)

of humans?"[160] Here Gandhi reminds us of Plato's idea of art as imitation.[161] But when it comes to the music Gandhi responds differently as he says: "To me music is something to receive joy and inspiration from." and reminisces by saying that "how well I remember, the joy and peace and comfort that music used to give me when I was ailing in a South African hospital. I was then recovering from some hurts I had received at the hands of some roughs who had been engaged to cripple me—thanks to the growing success of my passive Resistance Campaign. At my request the daughter of a friend of mine used, very often, to sing to me the famous hymn, *Lead Kindly Light.* And how it acted like a healing balm—invariably! I still remember this song with gratitude."[162] No wonder music and prayer became the integral part of his well-structured daily chores and scheme of things that he never missed even on busy schedule of his foreign trips. Here is Louis Fischer reporting Gandhi's stay with Romain Rolland in Switzerland after returning from Round Table Conference at London in Dec'1931: "The last evening Gandhi asked Rolland to play some Beethoven. Rolland played the Andante from the fifth symphony and, as an encore of his own accord, Gluck's *Elysian Fields.* The theme of the Fifth Symphony is considered to be man's struggle with fate, man's harmony with fate, the brotherhood of man. The second movement, the Andante, is melodious and suffused with tender lyrical emotions, quiet nobility and optimism. Rolland chose it because it came closest to his concept of Gandhi's personality. It is gentle and loving. In the Gluck piece one almost hears the angels singing to the strains of the flute. It

---

160 Ibid, P.300 (ibid, pp.61–67)

161 Plato, Republic, (Tr.C.D.C. Reeve), Hackett Publishing, 2004

162 Shriman Narayan, Ibid, p297 (ibid)

is celestial music, full of purity and clarity. The Gita might be set to it."[163] This incidence was also noted by Rolland himself in his diary that Gandhi expressly wanted him to play Beethoven and after playing he writes, "when we ask for his impression, replies with a mischievous and candid little laugh: "it must be good since you say so!"[164] In fact, Gandhi pleaded several times that he prefers the art and literature that can speak to the millions. Certainly, Gandhi was all for 'communication' and not for 'expression' in Art. Citing the example of Dean Farrar' book on the life of Christ he reported that the writer had read "everything about Jesus in the English language, and then he went to Palestine, saw every place and spot in the Bible that he could identify, and then wrote the book in faith and prayer, for the masses in England, in a language which all of them could understand. It is not in Dr. Johnson's style but in the easy style of Dickens. Have we men like Farrar who will produce great literature for the village folk? Our literary men will pore on Kalidas and Bhavbhuti and English authors, and will give us imitations. I want them to go to villages, study them and give something life-giving...I want art and literature that can speak to the millions."[165] Gandhi always maintained that since we don't need an interpreter to enjoy the panoramic view of nature—the colour and feel of sunrise, the tranquil temper of the sunset or the cooling breeze of spring as it is communicated directly without any aid so he asks, "Why should I need an artist to explain a work of art to me? Why should it not speak out to me itself? I saw in the Vatican art-collection a statue of Christ on the cross which simply captured me and kept me spell-bound.

---

163 Luis Fischer, Ibid, p369.

164 Romain Rolland, ibid, p.212

165 Shriman Narayan, Ibid, p.304–305 (Harijan, 14-11-1936)

I saw it five years ago but it is still before me. In Belur in Mysore, I saw in the ancient temple a bracket in stone made of a little statuette, which spoke out to me without any one to help me to understand it. It was just a woman, half-naked, struggling with the folds of her clothes to extricate herself from the shafts of cupid, who is after all lying defeated at her feet in the shape of a scorpion. I could see the agony on the form—the agony of the stings of the scorpion.[166]

In the context of Gandhi's proposition of nature-like Art and its easy communicability, we can counter pose it into one of the illustration that Tagore had cited in a debate with Gandhi, he said, "I am in search of a *vina* player. I have tried East and I have tried West, but have not found the man of my quest. They are all experts, they can make the strings resound to a degree, they command high prices, but for all their wonderful execution they can strike no chord in my heart. At last I came across one whose very first notes melt away the sense of oppression within. In him is the fire of the Shakti of joy which can light up all other hearts by its touch. His appeal to me is instant and I hail him as Master. I then want a vina made. For this, of course are required all kind of material and a different kind of science. If, finding me to be lacking in the means my master should be moved to pity and say: "Never mind, my son do not go to the expense in workmanship and time which a vina will require. Take rather this simple string tightened across a piece of wood and practice on it. In a short time you will find it to be as good as a vina." Would that do? I am afraid not."[167]

---

166 Ibid, p291 (ibid, p315)

167 Sabyasachi Bhattacharya (ed.), The Mahatma and the Poet, National Book Trust, Delhi, second reprint 1999, p.80

Gandhi & Gandhism as Art-Subject

Gandhi and Gandhism has been explained, represented and interpreted, over the years in various art-forms—in literature, in Drama & theatre, in film, music, painting, sculpture and what not, even in parodies and computer games. By any account, it is a huge body of work and considering the limited space of an article, it is hardly possible to deal comprehensively, so we have to be selective in our approach.

Gandhi in Literature

There are very few icons like Gandhi in the world who have inspired and caught the imagination of so many people including artists, literatures, performers etc. on such a scale that is truly phenomenal and its momentum is still continuing; that's why the work on his personality and his various practices is growing day by day to such an extent that it is now impossible to even recount all in a single book, let alone in an article! So here, we confine ourselves to the arena of creative literature, i.e. selected novels, poems, plays etc. in which Gandhi is portrayed as a character or Gandhi is directly addressed or Gandhism or the issues raised by Gandhi was explored in any way[168]. Even this body of work is so impressive and far-reaching that most of the historiography of Indian literatures— including Indian English literature— classifies 1920s to independence as 'Gandhian age'. M.K.Naik writes in A History of Indian English Literature:

---

168 Though it can be argued that criticism is also part of creative literature but the body of critical writing (including biography and Memoirs) on Gandhi is so vast and huge that it goes beyond our scope ;even its bibliography runs in three volumes, see, M.Pandri (compiled) A comprehensive Annotated Bibliography on Mahatma Gandhi,3 volumes, Greenwood Press, 1995

"Indian English literature of the Gandhian age was inevitably influenced by these epoch –making developments (the freedom movement) in Indian life. A highly significant feature is the sudden flowering of the novel during the thirties, when the Gandhian movement perhaps was at its strongest....The work of K.S.Venkatramani, Mulk Raj Anand and Raja Rao would not perhaps have been possible had the miracle that was Gandhi not occurred during this period."[169] This miracle was not happening only in the arena of Indian English fiction but almost in all the genres and across the languages in India.

Kaveripatnam Siddhanatha Venkataramani (1891–1952) in *Murugan the Tiller* (1927) and *Kandan:The Patriot* (1932) and Raja Rao (1908–2006) in the novel *Kanthapura* (1938) and the collection of short stories titled *The Cow of the Barricades* (1947), envisaged the characters with Gandhian principles. So in the same way in *Untouchable* (1935), *Coolie* (1936), *Two Leaves and a Bud* (1937), *The Village* (1939) and *The Sword and the Sickle* (1942), Mulk Raj Anand (1905–2004) portrayed the principle characters through the vision of Gandhi and in two of his works Gandhi himself appeared briefly on some scenes. He was also depicted appearing on the scene in the novel *Waiting for the Mahatma* (1955) of R.K.Narayan (1906–2001) and Khawaja Ahmed Abbas's *Inquilab (1958)*. Manohar Malgonkar's *A band in the Ganges* (1964) examines the complexities of Gandhian era. Later, a very ambitious series of novels written by Chaman Nahal (1927–2013) appeared —its first volume called *Azadi* (Freedom) in 1975, 2nd volume *The Crown and the Loincloth* in 1981, 3rd *The salt of Life* in 1990 and the final sequel *The triumph of the Tricolor* in 1993.

---

169 M.K.Naik, A History of Indian English Literature, Sāhitya Akademi, New Delhi, 1982, p118

It was grand in scale and historical in its treatment covering the whole spectacular life journey of Mahatma Gandhi, reminding us Tolstoy's the great *War and Peace*. Shashi Tharoor's *The grand Indian Novel* (1989) parallels Mahabharata's Bhishm Pitamah to Gandhi and later in the Indian English fiction the emphasis gradually turned to focus Gandhi's inner world like Psycho-analyst Sudhir Kakar's novel The *Seeker* (2007), where Gandhi is depicted in some fictional and some not –so- fictional settings, based on letters, diaries, and autobiographical accounts to delineate his relationship with Madeline Slade (Meera Behn), a thirty three year old British woman who left her privileged life as an admiral's daughter and became disciple of Gandhi.

If we survey Hindi Literature of that point of time we find that almost all the major writers were influenced by the magnetic personality of Gandhi and his methods. In fiction Premchand (1880–1936), Bhagvaticharan Varma (1903–1981), Jainendra Kumar (1905–1988), Visambharnath Sharma 'Kaushik' (1899–1945), Sudarshan (1895–1967) were responding in some way to the Gandhian principles or his ways of perception. The protagonist of *Rangbhoomi (1924)* Surdas practices Satyagraha; when his friends are about to resort to violence, he says: "Bhaiyyon, go to your homes. I'm requesting you with folded hands to go home. Where's the point of assembling here and annoying the authorities? If death comes to me, you people will just remain standing and I'll die. If death doesn't come to me, I'll escape, protecting myself from the mouths of the cannons. Actually you people haven't come to help me but to show your enmity. You have turned the thoughts of mercy and dharma that would have come to the minds of the authorities, of the army, of the police, into anger by assembling here."[170] This is very obvious that it is the language Gandhi spoke all through his life. Premchand took yet another Gandhian concept of heart-transformation in the novel Premashram (1922) and again he contextualizes the story of *Karmabhoomi (1932)* in the Gandhian civil- disobedience movement. Gandhi as a full-fledged character is to be found later in novel like Giriraj Kishore's *Pahla Girmitia (1999)* but different facets of Gandhism has been dealt in so many novels like Jainendra Kumar's *Sunita (1936)*, Bhagvaticharan Varma's *Tedhe Medhe Raste (1946)*, Phanishwar Nath Renu (1921–1977)'s *Maila Aanchal (1954)* and so on. Ageya writes about Jainendra Kumar, "He gave creative expression to the Gandhian Philosophy of passive resistance boldly carrying it to the logical extreme of non-resistance to evil and acceptance of suffering."[171] The same way in Gujarati there were two groups of writers, one group belonged to Kaka Kalelkar, Ramnarayan Pathak, Kishorelal Mashruwala who inculcated Gandhian principles and made their main theme of the work and second group was influenced by Gandhi but they adopted independent line. K.M. Munshi's (1887–1971)'s novel *Swapnadrashta* deals with the independence movement and Similarly in Marathi, Vaman Malhar Joshi (1883–1943)'s novel *Indu Kale Sarla Bhole* (1925) the main character Sarla is the wife of a practicing Gandhian and S.R. Biwalkar's (1919–1972)'s famous novel *Suneeta* (1947) is centered around Noakhali riots and the background of Saratchandra Muktibodh (1921–1984)'s *Kshipra* is Quit India movement of 1942. Marathi novelists, Sane

---

170 Premchand, Playground (Rangbhoomi), Tr. Manju Jain, Penguin India, First Edition 2011, p.575

171 Contemporary Indian Literature: A Symposium, Sāhitya Akademi, New Delhi 2nd edition 1959, P.90

Guruji (Kranti, God Shevat, Astik and Nava Prayog) and Prema Kantak (Kam ani Kamini and Agni-Yan) were also known for their Gandhi-novels. These novels deals with the historical moments of our country that are invariably associated with Gandhi and his times. Though Gandhi's life and teachings were very influential in Kannada literary sphere, it seems, the fiction were not very conducive for its propogation;however some novels of V.K. Gokak, Basawraj Kattimani, Inamdar, T.R.Subba Rau, Gorur Rameswami Aiyangar, Kota Shivarama Karanth may be termed as Gandhian. The situation in Tamil fiction was different since the writers of *Manikkodi group* were very active propagating Gandhian values and it is estimated that 'in a period of ten years at least a thousand books inspired by Gandhism were published in Tamil. A women writer V.M. Kodainayaki Ammal wrote more than a hundred novels in which the Gandhian impact is obvious.'[172] Kalki Krishnamurthy (1899–1954)'s *Alai Osai* depicts hard and turbulent times of thirties and forties through the eyes of a common man.it was a kind of novelist's tribute to the father of the nation. In Orissa, Gopabandhu Das (1877–1928) who was an active participant in the non-cooperation movement always depicted in his work the Gandhian ideals and Kalindi Charan Panigrahi (1901–1991) his junior but equally famous compatriot depicted in his seminal novel *Matira Manisha* (1966) like Premchand the Gandhian belief in change of heart. In Bangla fiction, the Gandhian influence is very much evident in the work of Tarashankar Bandopadhyaya (especially, Dhatridevata), Satinath Bhaduri (Jagari, dhodhai charit manas), Anandsankar Ray (Satyasatya), Banphool, Manoj Basu, Nabendu Ghosh,

---

172 Bhabani Bhattacharya, Gandhi the writer, National Book Trust, Delhi, 1969, P.237

Sumathnath Ghosh, Gajendra Kumar Mitra, Subodh Ghosh and others. Tarashankar Bandopadhyaya was actively involved in the freedom struggle led by Gandhi and his hero in *Dhatridevata* declares, "This struggle is, indeed, unique. You don't have to kill, you will have to die. This is a war without arms, Bare-handed, you stand fearless before the guns pointed at your body."[173] Similarly first novel—*Jagari* — of Satinath Bhaduri describes freedom struggle and Gandhian way of life; the translator of this novel (The Vigil) in English writes in introduction, "The vigil is the first novel in Bengal to be written against the political and social background of the 1942 movement...it was written in 1944, the year Gandhi was released from prison, and published in 1946, a few months before India was formally declared a free and independent nation...it is safe to say that a novel of this kind could not have been either written or published earlier."[174] Definitely the influence of Gandhi is not so meagre on Bangla literature that it can be overlooked and ignored. Working on the Bangla literary journals Sarvani Gooptu writes, "The 35 essays and poems published between 1916–1939 in Bangabani, Bharati, Bharatvarsha, Bichitra and Prabashi, and the newspaper Ananda Bazar Patrika, which followed the Tagore-Gandhi relationship between (1922–1932) coinciding with the prime time of the Gandhian movements in India reflect a Bengali viewpoint frequently ignored in discussions on the subject.

"Gandhi's relationship with Bengal began much before he became the Mahatma, starting with an article he sent for translation and publication in Bharati in 1902 on Indian

---

173 Ibid, p.235

174 Ibid, pp. 235–236

Colonisation in South Africa. From 1921, regular poems and essays appeared — some in uncomplicated admiration of his persona, ideal of Satyagraha and hope for the future through poems by Satyendranath Dutta, Hemendralal Roy, Pyarimohan Sen Gupta's Gandhi Bandana, and other poems on khadi and charkha including the famous song of Charkha by Kazi Nazrul Islam, and an article on the Salt March to Dandi by an enthusiastic volunteer from Bolpur, Akshoy Kumar Roy (Bichitra, 1931)."[175] Discussing the impact of Gandhi on Indian literature, Sisir Kumar Das writes, "The advent of Gandhi in Indian life, profound and pervasive in impact, spectacular and dramatic in form, must be considered as one of the most memorable phenomena in the history of Indian Literature...Gandhi became the theme of the new patriotic-nationalistic poetry that emerged after the advent of Gandhi in Indian politics...Satyendranath Datta wrote in the beginning of 1921: *Lo, harken to the uproar on the city street/billowing, Gandhiji, Gandhiji.*"[176]

This new patriotic-nationalistic poetry became the major trend in almost all the languages of India at that point of time; Whether it is poetry of Ambika Giri Raichoudhury or Kanak Chandra Sarma in Assamese or Meghani, Umashankar Joshi, Sneharashmi in Gujarati or Dattatraya Ramchandra Bendre or Masti venkatesha Aiyangar in Kannada or Radhamohan Gadanayak in Orriya, or Vallathol and Shankar Kurup in Malayalam or Ramalingam and V. Kalyansundaranar in Tamil or Krishna Shastri and Basavraju Appa Rao in Telugu or Chakbast

---

175 https://www.nationalheraldindia.com/india/gandhi-and-bengal-a-complicated-relationship (accessed on 29.09.2022)

176 Sisir Kumar Das, A History of Indian Literature, 1911–56, Sahitya Akademi, Delhi, First Published 1995, Pp.64–65

and Akbar Allahabadi in Urdu and Ayodhya Singh Upadhyay *Harioudh*, Maithilisharan Gupta or Sohanlal Dwivedi in Hindi or for that matter —Sarojini Naidu and others in English— all these poets were vibrating with patriotic Gandhian nationalism. Sarojini Naidu, portrayed Gandhi as an eternal lotus: "O mystic Lotus, sacred and sublime/ In myriad-petalled grace inviolate/ Supreme o'er transient storms of tragic Fate/ Deep-rooted in the waters of all Time..."[177]

In Malayalam poetry, *Ente Gurunathan (1924)* is one of the most popular poems that is a kind of hymn of a disciple in praise of his master Gandhi Ji: "The country that the Gita bore/alone could bear a seer like him/who to *karma's* precepts betakes; the land that lies betwixt the arms/of Vindhyas and the Himavant/ alone could rear a lion like him/which to ascetic peace doth take;/the land through which the Ganga flows/alone could raise the *kalpaka*/which yields for man eternal good."[178] Similarly in Urdu, Pundit Brijnarayan *Chakbast* (1882–1926) wrote a poem in 1913 eulogizing Gandhi's struggle against racial discrimination in south Africa, titled "Fariyad-e-qaum" (The complaint of the nation): "Samajh Liya hai ki hame ranj-e-dard sahena hain/ Magar zaban se kahenge wahi jo kahna hai (Realized that we have to live with pain and anguish/ But we will utter only what we want to say). A prominent Urdu critic Ali Ahmad Fatimi in his brilliantly documented article "Gandhiji in Urdu literature" points out that the first national poet of Urdu, *Chakbast*, was highly impressed by the crusade against racial discrimination that he launched in South Africa. The poet makes a fervent

---

177 Sarojini Naidu, The Broken Wing, William Heinemann, lLondon, 1917, p.29

178 P.K.Parameshwaran Nair, History of Malayalam Literature, (English Translation from Malayalam by E.M. J. Venniyoor), Sahity Akademi, 1958, p.204

plea "Watan se hain Tu door par nigah kar laina/idhar bhi aag lagi hai zara khabar kar laina" (Though you are away from the country/ Fire engulfs us do take care of!) It was probably the first verse addressed to Gandhi.[179] Extra-ordinary Urdu poet Akbar Allahabadi wrote *Gandhinama,* asserting to compose an epic on an inspiring Indian personality instead of taking inspiration from *Shahnama*. Taking this clue, there were so many Urdu poems were composed by poets like Zafar Ali Khan, Hasrat Mohani, Mohammad Ali Jauhar, Majaz, Josh Maliabadi, Asar Lucknawi, Jan Nisar Akhtar, Anand Narian Mulla, Wamiq Jaunpuri, Iqbal Suhail and Jameel Mazhari etc.[180]

In Hindi, too, poets responded to Gandhian philosophy enthusiastically resulting in a new kind of patriotic-nationalistic poetry as noted Hindi critic Ramswaroop Chaturvedi rightly pointed out that in Hindi, the renaissance has connected spirituality to the public service and then public service to nationalism[181] and it can be testified in the works of poets like Ajodhya Singh Upadhyay *Harioudh (Priyapravas:1914)*, Gokul Chandra Sharma (*Gandhi Gaurav:1919)* Maithilisharan Gupta (*Saket 1932*), Gaya Prasad Shukla *Sanehi,* Sohanlal Dwivedi (1906–1988) (*Yugavatar Gandhi)*, Shiyaram Sharan Gupta (*Bapu 1938),* Mohanlal Mahto *Viyogi (Aryavarta:1943)* Ramcharit Upadhyay, Sridhar Pathak, Ramnaresh Tripathi, Ramdhari Singh *Dinkar* (Bapu: 1947), Dulerai Karani *(Gandhi Bawani:1948)* Raghuvir sharan *Mitra (Jannayak:1949)* Sumitranandan Pant & Harivansh

---

179 https://www.thehindu.com/books/books-authors/gandhi-in-urdu-literature/article28708422.ece(accessed on 18.09.2022)

180 See, Syed Moazzam Ali (ed.) Nakhlistan, Rajasthan Urdu Academy, Jaipur, 2019.

181 Ramswaroop Chaturvedi, Hindi Sāhitya aur Samvedana ka Vikas, Lokbharati Prakashn, Allahabad, p.103

Rai *Bachchan* (*Khadi Ke Phool:1948*) , Gopal Sharan Singh (*Jagadalok:1952*), Sumitranandan Pant (Lokayatan:1963), Bhavani Prasad Mishra (*Gandhi Panchsati: 1969*) etc. No wonder when Sohalnlal Dwivedi edited an poetry anthology of representative poets on Gandhi under *Gandhi Abhinandan Granth* on the eve of Gandhi Ji's seventieth Birth celebration, fifty (50) Hindi poets were included whereas Urdu had fifteen (15), Bangla Twelve (12), Marathi Twelve (12), Gujarati eleven (11), English eleven (11), Telgu Five (5), Kannad Four (4), Orriya Three (3)), Rajasthani Two (2), Sindhi Two (2), Tamil Three (3), Malayalam Two (2), Chinese Two (2) and Maithili had one (1) representative poet.[182] These representative poets depicted Gandhi and his historical role in freedom struggle with all its glory but apart from depicting Gandhi or Gandhism some Gandhian principle has also been adopted by some authors in their creative process itself. The critic of Hindi Literature argues that the most salient feature of Gandhi's life and philosophy has been his parsimoniousness, that is connected with his ideal of forbearance...nothing should be wasted and every little material should be used—that was his basic mantra. In this way Premchand, and its own way Maithilisharan Gupta and others adopted this ideal of parsimony in their creative-process. This is the reason the depiction of social reality in Premchand and others does not over- expand, does not go waste. This ideal is more rigorously adopted in his treatment of language where he squeezes it to its limits.[183] And if it is seen in even more exemplary way, it is evident in the works of drama.

182 Sohalnlal Dwivedi (ed.) Gandhi Abhinandan Granth, Gandhi Abhinandan Granth Karyalaya,Lucknow,1944

183 Ramswaroop Chaturvedi, Hindi Sāhitya aur Samvedana ka Vikas, Lokbharati Prkashan, Allahabad, Pratham Sanskaran, 1986, p.166

In Indian English, Bharati Sarabhai (1912–96) has composed two plays in the duration of nine years —first *The well of the people* in 1943 and second *Two Women* in 1952, comprising the Gandhian precepts of our social ills. K.S. Rangappa's *Gandhi's Sadhana* (1968), Asif Currimbhoy (1928–1994)'s *An Experiment with Truth* (1972), Lakhan Dev's *Murder at the Prayer* (1972) and S.K. Ojha's *Riding the Storm* (1990) are few examples where Gandhi and his times were interrogated. In all Indian languages, Marathi dramas had a long history of producing plays on the various dimensions and interpretations of Gandhi—right from the Krishnaji Prabhakar Khadilkar (1872–1948) to Saefat Khan's *Gandhi Aadva Yeto* (2013), Gandhi or Gandhism is the central theme of the play. B.V. Warerkar (*Apoorva Banga*l), Madhusudan Kalelkar (*Fifteenth of August*), D.N.Shikhare (*Vaisanav Jan*), Pradeep Dalvi (*Me Nathuram Godse Boltoy*), Ajit Dalvi (Gandhi *Virudh Gandhi*), Premanand Gajvi (*Gandhi aani Ambedkar*) are the most famous playwrights who dealt with the subject with their subjective and sometimes controversial perspectives.

In Malayalam, few plays are conceived under the Gandhian influence, such as Edasseri Govindan Nayar (1906–1974)'s *Kuttukrishi*, N. Krishna Pillai (1916–1988)*'s Anuranjanam*, K.Surendran (1921–1997)'s *The house of Lac* etc. Similarly in Kannada G.P. Rajaratnam (1909–1979)'s *Sambhavami Yuge Yuge*, in Assamese plays of Jyoti Prasad Agarwala (1903–1951)'s such as *Karengar Lagiri* (1937) *Rupalim (1938), Lobito (1945)* and few works of Atulchandra Hazarika (1903–86) and Satya Prasad Barua (1919–) can be cited but it is true that plays on Gandhi are relatively few and far between. Same is the case of Hindi drama where playwright like Hari Krishna Premi (1908–

74) and Seth Govind Das (1896–1974) wrote some plays like *Swarnavihaan* (1930), *Rakshabandhan* (1934), *Shiv Sadhana* (1937) and *Sevapath* respectively based on Gandhian Humanism even without Gandhian precepts Jaishankar Prasad (1889–1937)'s great protagonists Skandagupta, Devsena, Dhruvswamini perhaps were not possible, but in Hindi drama Gandhi as subject in general was not touched upon. Is it because Gandhi as subject of a play is not dramatic enough to sustain genre specific demands, as one scholar argued that: "His saintly image overtook his political career to disallow the intensity necessary to create conflicts on which the dramatic art thrives. His faith and beliefs were so absolute that they offered no room for any inner character conflict."[184] This formulation can be contested or debated, if we see George Orwell's reflections on Gandhi, that is quite different from it: "His character was an extraordinarily mixed one, but there was almost nothing in it that you can put your finger on and call bad, and I believe that even Gandhi's worst enemies would admit that he was an interesting and unusual man who enriched the world simply by being alive."[185]

In 1995, Feroz Abbas Khan staged the "Gandhi Virudh Gandhi" in Mumbai. This play was based on Dinkar Joshi's Guajarati Novel 'Prakashno Padchayo' (Shadows of Light) in which the troubled relationship of Gandhi with his elder son Harilal was explored. This was an effort to understand Gandhi not in the realm of Politics but in his private sphere. The play was staged in Marathi, Gujarati, Hindi and English (in English, titled Mahatma vs. Gandhi) and got rave reviews. As Gandhi,

---

184 O.P. Bhatnagar, The Image of Gandhi in Indian Plays in English, Indian Literature, July-August 1981, Vol 24, No. 4 , p.128

185 The Orwell Reader, Harcourt Brace and Company, New York, First Edition 1956, pp330–331

in different productions, Atul Kulkarni, Boman Irani and Nasseruddin Shah were able to delve deep into the psyche of a father who had constantly been encroached upon his private and public domain. The play was staged successfully across the country.

Next year, in Jan' 1996 Gandhi was presented in shadow puppetry. Commissioned by Sangeet Natak Akademi and Indira Gandhi National Centre for the Arts, three important episodes of Gandhi's life—train episode of South Africa, Dandi march and Swadeshi andolan were chosen by puppeteer Murugan Rao of Tamil Nadu to depict in the National Shadow Puppetry Festival at Dharmasthala, Karnataka. But as Salil Singh has reported, "Puppeteers in whose hands shadows of mythical heroes had danced and cavorted, accompanied by passionate songs and cascading music, suddenly found themselves struggling awkwardly with bland images of a national hero, uninspired and uninspiring. They tried valiantly to fulfill their commission, yet it was apparent that the "experiment" was revealing only the futility of this attempt to take this traditional art "forward."[186]

In recent times *Me Nathuram Godse Boltoy* (1989) and its reincarnation *Hey Ram...Nathuram (2016)* by Sharad Ponkshe and *Gandhi aani Ambedkar* attracted quite a lot of criticism and attention from the critic and the wider public in general. Some even protests and ban followed since "According to the protesters, the play glorifies Gandhi's assassin and ought to be banned. While critics don't endorse a ban, they do believe that Ponkshe's play is an obvious and worrying reiteration of the

---

186 Salil Singh, If Gandhi Could Fly...: Dilemma and Directions in Shadow Puppetry of India, The Drama Review, Vol.43, No.3, p154

Hindutva ideology that led to Gandhi's death in 1948."[187] This controversial play somehow justifies the Godse's action of killing as Gandhi was shown responsible for the partition of the country. It was a highly volatile and condemnable issue; no wonder after six shows it was banned but again permitted in 2002. Creating antithetical situation or anti-hero is a theatrical ploy but outright justification of an objectionable action (i.e. murder) reduces it to the level of propaganda. In this way, the play 'Gandhi-Ambedkar' (1997) by Premanand Gajvi has more potentiality. Directed by Chetan Datar and acted by Mangesh Bhide as Gandhi and Kishore Kadam as Ambedkar, the play tried to highlight the difference of opinions of two great souls, especially in the context of cast issue. Though the play is tilted towards Ambedkar it does not vandalize Gandhi either. It got some critical acclaim.

Reacting to the over-critical portrayal of Gandhi, some production started strengthening the proto-typical image of him. 'Mahadevbhai' (2002) is one such play that was based on the diary of Gandhi's secretary Mahadev Desai. Directed by Ramu Ramanathan, this play narrates the diary, effectively done by Jamini Pathak and in the course of it, throws light on some of the well-known, positive facts of mahatma's life. The play was staged across the country.

In 2005, a newly established Primetime Theatre Company, Mumbai had staged a two-act play of Pratap Sharma titled, 'Sammy! A Word that Broke an Empire'. The play was directed by Lillete Dube and Gandhi was enacted by Joy Sengupta (young

---

187 See,https://scroll.in/magazine/828114/on-stage-in-maharashtra-nathuram-godse-is-seeing-a-revival (accessed on 30.10.2022)

Gandhi) and Ravi Dube (Mahatma Gandhi).This play is two hour long and covers a long span of Gandhi's life—from South African days to last days, so consequently it is fast-paced and episodical. Although it does not go very deep into the psyche of the transformation of Gandhi to Mahatma, nevertheless it makes the text of Gandhism communicable to the youth and 'uninitiated.' After its premier at Tata Theatre NCPA, Mumbai on 30th July 2005 it was staged across the country and all over the world successfully.

In 2006, Mohan Maharishi presented Gandhi in a less-explored form in India called documentary theatre or docu-drama. This was the form that was mainly popularized by Heiner-Muller in the west, but Mohan Maharishi has used it bit differently, as he clarified later, "I could have, like Heiner-Muller, changed the facts of history and staged a very fictitious play. It was very tempting to do that. However, after my extensive research on the letters between Gandhi and Nehru, I have stuck to the facts."[188] Based on twenty two letters exchanged between Gandhi and Nehru, over the period of 21 years (1927–48), this innovative venture,'Dear Bapu' tried to capture the essence of one of the most turbulent period of our national history. Under the auspice of Vikram Sarabhai Foundation, the play was enacted in one hour forty five minutes in English at India Habitat Centre, Delhi. To link the references of the letter and make a single dramatic structure the director had used Sabina Mehta as narrator, besides Bhaskar Ghosh as Gandhi and Sunit Tondon as Nehru. It is obvious that director had no

---

188 Deccan Herald, Feb 3' 2008

desire for physical proximity in casting as he later elaborated: "All the words spoken in this play are of Gandhi and Nehru. But, Gandhi and Nehru are not impersonated here. There is Brechtian alienation. Ideas are important, not characters. I find it extremely annoying to enact Nehru, or, to impersonate or imitate Gandhi, because however good an actor one may be, as was Ben Kingsley in the film 'Gandhi', it does not help. The psycho-spiritual qualities of Gandhi's personality were missing in Kingsley's portrayal"[189] This is a point that could be debatable, nevertheless the performance made it convincing for such experimentation. Perhaps taking cue from it, M.K.Raina had staged 'Stay Yet Awhile' in 2007; based on the letters and debates between Gandhi and Tagore over the period of 1915 to 1941. This correspondence was compiled and edited by Prof. Sabyasachi Bhattacharya in a book titled 'The Mahatma and the Poet', in which he rightly pointed out that he "was struck by the significance of these letters in terms of the differing perceptions they had of major national issues, as well as the intimate light the letters throw upon the relationship between these two friends and adversaries in debate."[190] Apart from Gandhi (Dhruv Jagasia), and Tagore (Avijit Dutt) Raina has introduced Danish Hussain as sutradhar. The stage was designed in such a way that reading out of letters in the backdrop of documentary footages of national movement turned into a lively and interactive space. It was critically acclaimed and the show was repeated in various places across the country.

---

189 ibid

190 Sabyasachi Bhattacharya, ibid, preface

Gandhi as Writer

Gandhi's collected works run into hundred volumes containing fifty thousand pages, and it is edited written in between 1884 to 1948. By any account it is a huge body of work. He has written almost one lakhs letters and in the words of Anu Bandopadhyaya, "His urge to write made him scribble on running trains and rocking ships. He prepared the whole of the Green Pamphlet a while on voyage home in 1896. Hind Swaraj, a severe criticism of modern civilization, was written at stretch during his voyage from England to South Africa in 1909. He used the steamer stationary. When he got tired of writing with his right hand, he used the left and finished the books in ten days. Tolstoy read it and said that the question of passive resistance was 'of very great importance not only for India but for whole world.' Constructive Programme, a booklet on nation building work, was written on a train. His manuscripts had few marks of correction and seldom needed any change. Like in all other sphere, in the domain of writing also Gandhi does not preach a thing that he himself does not practice. If he says that literature must be simple in its presentation and direct in its expression like the language of Nature,"[191] his own writing is its biggest example—simple presentation and direct expression. See this one-liner: "Khadi is the sun of the village solar system."[192] Or this letter to Subhash Chandra Bose: *The views you express seem to me to be so diametrically opposed to those of the others and my own that I do not see any possibility of bridging them...What is wrong is not the difference between us but loss of mutual respect and trust.*

---

191 Anu Bandopadhyaya M. K. Gandhi: Author, Journalist, Printer, Navjivan Press, Ahmadabad, in (www, mkgandhi.org/j.a.p/author.htm)

192 Shriman Narayan, ibid, p398 (Harijan, 16.11.1934)

This will be remedied by time which is the best healer...My prestige does not count. It has an independent value of its own. When my motive is suspected or my policy or programme rejected by the country, the prestige must go. India will rise and fall by the quality of the sum total of her many millions. Individuals, however high they may be, are of no account except in so far as they represent the many millions."[193] This is what he means by simple presentation and direct expression: a crystal clear expression coming out of the habit of catching- by- horn kind of directness and this has made him one of the most effective letter-writer of his time. K.M. Munshi rightly pointed out that, "No man has wielded so great an influence through his letters; and few literary men have written theirs with such art. It is rarely that one comes across such an inimitable epistle as the one he wrote from the yervada jail to the children of the Sabarmati Ashram:

"Ordinary birds cannot fly without wings. With wings, of course, all can fly. But if you, without wings, will learn how to fly, then all your troubles will indeed be at an end. And I will teach you.

See, I have no wings, yet I come flying to you every day in thought. Look, here is little Vimala, here is Hari, and here Dharmakumar. And you also can come flying to me in thought.

There is no need of a teacher for those who know how to think. The teacher may guide us but he cannot give us the power of thinking. That is latent in us. Those who are wise get wise thoughts.

Tell me who, amongst you, are not praying properly in Prabhubhai's evening prayer.

---

193 Ibid, vol.5. pp.241–42

Send me a letter signed by all and those who do not know how to sign may make a cross.

Yervada Palace

Silence day.

Bapu's blessings.[194]

Gandhi has edited three journals. The first was *Indian Opinion* (1903–1915) that he started in South Africa, it was bilingual—in English & Gujarati and for a short period in Tamil and Hindi too. The other two: *Young India* (1919–1932) in English, (its Gujarati version was 'Navajivan') and *Harijan* (1933–1948) in Gujarati, Hindi and English all from Ahmadabad. B.R.Nanda has rightly pointed out that: "Gandhi's journals were read by his political opponents and by the British officials as well as the Congress leaders because Gandhi used his journals for loud thinking. As Louis Fischer once said Gandhi did not have a blue pencil; he made few revisions, he wrote as thoughts came to him. The importance of the journals edited by Gandhi-Indian Opinion, Young India, Navajivan and Harijan – is that he used them to propagate his views through persuasion, discussion and debate. He opened up the columns of these journals even to his critics. He published their criticisms and then answered them. Once Jamnalal Bajaj complained that the Mahatma gave more time to his critics than to his adherents; Gandhi answered that he did not have to convert the converted and preferred to listen to his critics to try to remove their doubts."[195] A professor at the Oxford University, who assisted on drafting some of Gandhi's

---

194 K.M. Munshi, Gujarata and its Literature, Longmans Green & Co.Ltd.Calcutta, 1935, pp.316–317

195 B.R. Nanda, www.mkgandhi.org

statements made at the Round Table Conference, said: "I have never met an Indian who had mastered the prepositions as Gandhi has.... I took a deal of trouble over this drafting. Mr. Gandhi would glance over my work and would make just one suitable prepositional change. It did its work. It changed my meaning into Mr. Gandhi's meaning."[196]

It is important to note that all significant work of Gandhi is written in Gujarati– Be it Hind Swaraj (1909), or Satyano Prayogo (My Experiments with Truth 1927 & 1929) or Dakshin Africana Satyagramo Itihas (Satyagraha in South Africa, 1924) or for that matter his Discourses on Gita (1930). And these are the work that pioneered in Gujarati prose a style that is bereft of any ornamental vagueness or pseudo-abstractness and clearly it marks a departure. This was the style that captures truth while it resonates and critics called it 'Gandhian style.' No wonder with Narmada Shankar, Mansukh Ram Tripathi, Naval Ram and K.M. Munshi, he is considered to be the pioneer of modern Gujarati prose. K.M. Munshi states that "Mahatma Gandhi has given to Gujarati prose a new sense of power. His vocabulary has been drawn from many sources. His style, though sometimes loosely woven in construction, its direct, clear and easily comprehensible, the result of precise thinking and an incessant effort to avoid the devious by-paths of rhetoric and sophistry. An unerring sense of proportion keeps both expression and imagination under judicious restraint. The literary element is always subordinated to the author's prime motive, which is to

---

196 Quoted in Anu Bandopadhyaya, ibid.

touch the living chord in the reader's heart and vivify him into action."[197]

Gandhi has contributed in another way also to improve the quality of Gujarati prose is by doing some translation in Gujarati. He has translated Ruskin's 'unto this last', Plato's 'Defense and Death of Socrates', 'Life of Kamal Pasha' and some work of Carlyle into Gujarati. His was not a literal translation, rather very consciously text was adopted to the demand of an emerging prose; this is the reason why 'Unto This Last' became 'Sarvodaya' and 'Defense and Death of Socrates' into 'Satyavir Sokritis'. Gandhi has also translated some devotional work of medieval saint poets into English. Gandhi was also very concerned about the moral upliftment of children and a lack of reading material for them so like in all other sphere he himself set an example; he wrote two books for them—one primer called, 'Balpothi' and other 'Nitidharma'. It was his well thought idea that "if we are to reach real peace in this world and if we are to carry on war against war, we shall have to begin with children; and if they will grow up in their natural innocence, we won't have to struggle, we won't have to pass fruitless idle resolutions. But we shall go from love to love and peace to peace, until at last all the corners of the world are covered with that peace and love for which, consciously or unconsciously, the whole world is hungering."[198]

In some way, it is true that not only 'Balpothi' or 'Nitikatha' but whole of the Gandhi –oeuvre helps us to grow in our *natural innocence!*

---

197 K.M.Munshi, ibid,p.312

198 Shriman Narayan, ibid, pp.495-96(Young India, 19.11.1931, p361).

Gandhi in Films

It is no secret that Gandhi not only disliked films, but put it with other vices like 'race-course, drink-booth and opium-den' as the "enemies of the society."[199] and in one place during a conversation with Jayaprakash Narayan and others, Gandhi said, "If I had my way, I would see to it that all the cinemas and theatres in India were converted in to spinning halls and factories of handicrafts of all kind."[200] So it is interesting and somehow ironical that his disdain towards cinema could not prevent the film industry from making not only films on him but also using his name and his values — directly or indirectly — for propagating their commercial ventures. Sometimes it was done by simply putting a short documentary on Gandhi in the middle of a film, as is evident in the following advertisement of the 1933 film *Chintamani*, where its promotional write-up goes like this: "*Talkie film of a speech Mahatma Gandhi gave at Azad Maidan, which has been exclusively produced by Krishna Company. Also running is the film of his great reception from steamer Pilsna to Mani Bhavan. Do come with family to have the privilege of Mahatmaji's darshan and listen to his clear speech.*"[201]

Filming Gandhi in a systematic way has started with A. Karuppan Chettiar (1911–1983) who initiated making a documentary on him in 1937. He collected 50, 000 feet of film footage from India, London, and South Africa including his own filmed contemporary scenes of Gandhi. Eventually it was

---

199 Collected Works of Mahatma Gandhi, Vol.40, Page 125, 10 March 1929,

200 Collected Works of Mahatma Gandhi, Vol.88, Page 17, 27 May 1947.

201 See, https://theprint.in/opinion/heres-how-indian-films-of-the-1930s-and-1940s-used-gandhi-in-their-ads/296271/(accessed on 18.09.2022)

edited and 12,000 feet of documentary film called *Mahatma Gandhi: Twentieth Century Prophet* was released on 23 August 1940. It received good coverage from the Indian press and a few international newspapers like The New York Times. The documentary originally had voice-overs in Tamil and was later dubbed into Telugu. The film was stopped after the initial screening as it was found not suitable for public viewing by the colonial censorship. After Indian independence, the documentary was dubbed into Hindi and re-released in 1947.[202]

After Gandhi Ji's assassination in 1948 so many films in the west were announced but Hollywood's *Nine Hours to Rama* was the first film that released in 1963. The film depicted the nine hours in the life of Nathuram Godse that lead up to Gandhi Ji's assassination. Starring J.S. Casshyap as Gandhi, Horst Buchholz as Godse, Jairaj as G.D. Birla, Basdeo Pandey, (who later became Prime Minister of Trinidad and Tobago) in a minor role and filmed almost entirely on location in India, this film was directed and produced by Mark Robson (1913–78), based on the work of Historian Stanley Wolpert (1927–2019). The high point of the film was its ability to capture the tension and drama of the historical situation and resonance of a great human tragedy through soulful score of Malcom Arnold but on the other hand it also trivializes the very core of the same human tragedy. Godse became Hero and film turned into "A heady concoction of a little history and too much fiction, the film is a thriller full

---

202 Chettiar remembered some of his experiences in making this documentary in a series of articles in his own edited Tamil magazine Kumari Malar in 1943. These articles were eventually published in a book called Annal Adichuvattil (In the footsteps of the Mahatma). Kalachuvadu Publications Pvt Ltd, Revised and Expanded 2nd Edition, 2016

of romance rendered in a melodramatic mode."[203] No wonder it evoked strong reaction in India and subsequently first feature film on the father of the nation was also banned.

The second important venture in which Gandhi was portrayed in documentary form is *Mahatma: Life of Gandhi, 1869–1948*. The five hour long film was produced by The Gandhi National Memorial Fund in cooperation with the Films Division of India in 1968. It was based on newsreel, old archival materials and prints in various languages. This black and white 33 reels film was directed and scripted by Vithalbhai Jhaveri (1916–1985) who has also given commentary throughout this film. There are several versions of the film— There is one 5 hour version in English, another shorter version which runs for 2 hours and 16 minutes, and an even shorter version which runs for an hour are also available. A German version that runs for 1 hour and 44 minutes and a Hindi version of 2 hours and 20 minutes also exists.

It is generally considered the most complete feature film on Gandhi to this date is Richard Attenborough's 1982 classic *Gandhi* .Starring Ben Kingsley as Gandhi, Rohini Hattangadi as Kasturba Gandhi, Roshan Seth as Jawaharlal Nehru, Saeed Jaffrey as Sardar Vallabhbhai Patel, Alyque Padamsee as Jinnah and Written by John Briley, music composed by Ravi Shankar and George Fenton, this 188 minutes long film was a real spectacle costing $22, 000, 000. It turned out to be a huge success as it won eight Academy Awards, besides awards from BAFTA, National Board of Review and Golden Globes.

---

203 Ravinder Singh, Of Gandhi, Godse and the Missing Files: Nine Hours to Rama (1963), Economic and Political Weekly, Vol. 51, No. 30 (JULY 23, 2016), pp. 69

Generally, this film is considered to be historically correct but as far as the portrayal of the protagonist is concerned it was suggested from some quarters that Gandhi is over-idealized here and it is simply hagiography.[204] But approach of the film was quite clear from the very beginning as it opened with these words: "No man's life can be encompassed in one telling... least of all Gandhi's, whose passage through life was so entwined with his nation's struggle for freedom. There is no way to give each event its allotted weight, to recount the deeds and sacrifices of all the great men and women to whom he and India owe such immense debts. What can be done is to be faithful in spirit to the record of his journey, and to try to find one's way to the heart of the man..."Mostly the film justifies its opening claim though it can be argued as to how far the western-realist mode of the film and its flamboyant grand style is suitable for a subject like 'Gandhi'. Keeping this view in mind, noted Indian director Shyam Benegal had made a film titled *The Making of the Mahatma* in 1996 on Gandhi ji's twenty one years life in South Africa. Based on Fatima Meer's book *The Apprenticeship of a Mahatma* this film was a joint venture of NFDC India and SABC of South Africa. Starring Rajit Kapoor as Gandhi, Pallavi Joshi as Kasturba and Shot in actual locations of South Africa where Gandhi actually lived, including his old home at Loop Street; this 144 minutes long film succeeded to capture the very essence and process of becoming of a nineteen year old shy, timid advocate to an ever-growing, evolved person of forty.

---

204 "The film ...is pure hagiography; the late-twentieth-century equivalent of a medieval encomium of a remarkable saint rendered in words and illuminated pictures." James Lawrence, Raj: The Making and Unmaking of British India, Little Brown and company, p.465

Based on the letters written by Mahatma Gandhi to the Nazi German dictator Adolf Hitler, the film *Dear Friend Hitler (Hitler to Gandhi)*, released in 2011. Directed by Rakesh Ranjan Kumar and produced by Anil Kumar Sharma starring Raghuvir Yadav as Adolf Hitler, Neha Dhupia as Eva Braun and Avijit Dutt as Gandhi, this film could not communicate the intended moral superiority of non-violence over violence.

The film *Mohandas* a biographical film on Gandhi's childhood was released on his 150th birth anniversary. Based on Kannada writer Bolwar Mahammad Kunhi's story *Bapu Gandhi Aada Kathe.* (The Story of Mahatma Gandhi) and the autobiography of Mahatma Gandhi *My Experiments with Truth*, the film is scripted and directed by P. Sheshadri and it was released in three languages— English, Hindi and Kannada simultaneously in 2019. The film covers the events of Gandhi's childhood from the ages of 6 to 14. The role of Gandhi as a child was done by Param Swamy and Samarth Hombal as a teenager Gandhi. The film is successful in communicating not only the children audience but to all, the vital truths about life through the six years of child-life of a most innovative person of nineteenth century.

In 2012, A. Balakrishnan directed *Mudhalvar Mahatma (Welcome Back Gandhi)* was released in Tamil and English. Later it was released in Hindi too. This film tries to anticipate Gandhi's possible reaction towards the crisis of today's India including Ram janmabhoomi crisis. The movie seems credible by the music of Ilaiyaraaja, lyrics by Bharat Acharya and acting by S. Kanagaraj as Gandhi and Anupam Kher as a Chief Minister .

Hollywood's *The Gandhi Murder* is a 2019 historical political thriller film directed by Karim Traidia and Pankaj Sehgal.

It examines the events leading to the assassination of Mahatma Gandhi. This film focuses only on the last days of Mohandas Karamchand Gandhi that leads to his assassination and idea this film wants to project is that Hindu nationalist Godse was assisted by the govt.higher-ups in his elimination of Gandhi, so newly independent, fractured nation could unite. This far-fetched idea further seems unbelievable by the characterization of Gandhi played by Spaniard Jesus Sans. Another biographical drama movie about the Assassination of Mahatma Gandhi was made in 2017 called *Why I killed Gandhi*, but it was released on an OTT platform on 30th January'2022. Directed by Ashok Tyagi, Written and Produced by Kalyaani Singh, This 45 minutes short film is based on the arguments Nathuram Godse provided for killing Gandhi during his trials in the court. Amol Kolhe, the NCP Lok Sabha MP has played the role of Nathuram Godse. The film has flavour of Propaganda films.

Apart from these above-mentioned films, Gandhi had also been portrayed in the films where his contemporaries are the main protagonists like M.A. Jinnah ('Jinnah' 1998 dir.Jamil Dehlavi, Sam Dastor as Gandhi), Vallabhbhai patel ('Sardar', 1993, dir.Ketan Mehta, Anu Kapur as Gandhi), Vinayak Damodar Savarkar ('Veer Savarkar'2001, dir.Ved Rahi, Surendra Rajan as Gandhi), Baba Sahib Ambedkar ('Dr.Babasaheb Ambedkar', 2000, dir. Jabbar Patel, Mohan Gokhle as Gandhi) and Subhash Chandra Bose ('Neta Ji Subhash Chandra Bose: The Forgotten Hero '2005, dir.Shyam Benegal, Surendra Rajan as Gandhi). These films deserve separate elaboration but One thing can be emphasized here about these films is their inability to justify the protagonist's historical space in relation to Gandhi. Some films, like Hey Ram (dir.Kamal Hasan, 2000, Nasseruddin Shah as Gandhi), Water (dir.Deepa Mehta, 2005, Mohan jhangiani as Gandhi), Lage Raho Munnabhai (dir.Rajkumar Hirani, 2006, Dilip Prabhavalkar as Gandhi), were also made where Gandhi appeared briefly or film like Gandhi, My Father, based on the work of Chandulal Bhagubhai Dalal's Harilal Gandhi: A Life (dir.Feroz Abbas Khan, 2007, Darshan Jariwala as Gandhi) probes some less known, unexplored aspects of interpersonal relationship of Gandhi. Jahnu Barua's Maine Gandhi Ko Nahin Mara (2005) and Ketan Mehta's Mangal Pandey:The Rising (2005) uses some real footage of Gandhi for the purpose of story and its authenticity.

Gandhism in Films

It is difficult to differentiate Gandhi from Gandhism as Gandhi himself once famously remarked that his life is his message; but it is true that some films were made in which Gandhi was not portrayed but some components of Gandhism were dealt with. One film critic rightly pointed out that *The Mahatma's impact was evident in the works of Phalke, Shantaram, Mehboob Khan, Raj Kapoor, Hirani etc. The films dealt with the core themes of Gandhian ideology —— non-violence, love and sacrifice, Hindu-Muslim unity, the rural-urban divide, rejection of crass commercialism, women's emancipation and fear of moral decay. It was through their movies that Gandhi emerged as a towering moral force. While these filmmakers may not have imbibed his ideas consciously, their films revealed his influence, all the same, and it became a guarantee for success. Gandhism was, after all, too dominant an idea for idealistic filmmakers not to be swayed by it.*[205]

The first Tamil-Telugu Talking picture Kalidas (1931) that was released just few months after the first Indian talkie *Aalam Ara*, had one song of Madurai Bhaskara Das, sung by T.P. Rajalakshmi: *Raattinamaam Gandhi Kai baana maam.* Arguably this is perhaps first film song where Gandhi ji's name was mentioned. V.Shantharam (1901–90)'s film *Mahatma (1935)* had the hero resembling Gandhiji, so the British had him change the title to Dharmatma. His next film Amar *Jyoti* (1936) questioned the patriarchal norms and raised the women issue and *Dunia Na Mane* (1937) and *Dr.Kotnis ki Amar Kahani* (1946) can also be cited as testimonies of Gandhian influence. Like Shantaram, K.Subrahmanyam (1904–71) was also one of the earliest filmmakers to make films in support of the virtues Gandhi propagated. In 1936 he made *Balayogini* a Tamil film that attacked the Caste system, and next in 1938 he made Munshi Premchand's *Sevasadan* that dealt with the question of Prostitutes and the emancipation of women in India. His next film in 1939 was based on Kalki Krishnamurthy's famous novel *Tyagabhoomi.* This novel was clearly echoing Gandhi's call for Freedom and consequently was banned by the colonial government.

The social climate in the country brought about by Gandhi's movement against untouchability inspired many filmmakers to make socially relevant films. One such film was *Achhut Kanya* (1936) of Franz Osten (1876–1956) another was Chandulal

---

205 See, https://www.orfonline.org/expert-speak/gandhi-great-influencer-on-hindi-cinema-despite-his-celluloid-aversion-56035/(accessed on 11.4.2022)

Shah's *Achhut* (1940) in Hindi and Gujarati, where question of untouchability was raised sensibly and with the insight of Gandhi. Mehboob Khan's Aurat (1940) is another example where identity of women was established and its remake as *Mother India* (1957) reinforces it more strongly the agency of women in contemporary India. Raj Kapoor (1924–1988)'s early directorial ventures such as *Barsaat* (1949) *Awaara* (1951), *Shree* 420 (1955) where he created for himself a Charlie Chaplin like tramp persona has some trait of Gandhian simplicity. It may be safely argued that socially relevant films made in the 40s and early fifties certainly had some Gandhian influences. The relevance of Gandhism or rather lack of it for our contemporary Indian society is being hotly discussed. Ashutosh Gowariker's Swadesh (2004) opens with these words of Gandhi: "Hesitating to act because the whole vision might not be achieved, or because others do not yet share it, is an attitude that only hinders progress." It is said that the film director was inspired by the Rajni Bakshi's book 'Bapu Kuti' through which he came to know about the story of Arvind Pillalamarri and Ravi Kuchimanchi, the NRI couple who returned to India to develop the pedal power generator for impoverished rural sector. Tushar Gandhi has rightly pointed out that, "The film epitomizes Gandhi's value. Unfortunately it was like a documentary. It didn't get the box office success it deserved. It should've been less sermonizing, more humorous. I told Gowariker that *Swadesh* should be shown in every educational institution."[206] The same way Jahnu Barua has examined the lack of interest or apathy towards Gandhism in our society in the film *Maine Gandhi Ko Nahin Mara* (2005).

---

206 Tushar Gandhi, I'm pleased with Hirani's Gandhigiri, 19-03-2007, in www.nowrunning.com

But the film that has redefined the term Gandhism and acquired wide popularity was Raj Kumar Hirani's 2006 venture *Lage Raho Munnabhai*. Not only for its neologism 'Gandhigiri' but its queer and in some way very innovative mixing of comedy with Gandhian praxis has made this film quite a cult and controversial. That's why if it was criticized by saying that this "film trivializes Gandhi"[207] and "Gandhian philosophy is serious business and *Lage Raho Munna Bhai* is not the right way to show it."[208]; it was also hailed as 'never-done-before' kind of film: "True, there have been memorable films on Mahatma Gandhi by distinguished directors, namely Richard Attenborough and Shyam Benegal; one offering a respectful cinematic acquaintance and the other being didactic but inspiring. For all their earnestness, neither film stirred the popular imagination like LRM has done now."[209]

Gandhi in Parodies

The MTV cartoon 'Clone High' depicts the clone of Gandhi as one of the main characters. The Family Guy movie features a cutaway of a portrayed Gandhi unsuccessfully doing stand-up comedy at a club. The cartoon 'Time Squad' on Cartoon Network has an episode where Gandhi is portrayed as wanting to do tap dancing as a career, instead of leading India to independence. In the TV-show 'Scrubs Dr.Cox' constantly refers to Donald Faisons character as 'Gandhi'. A gun-toting Gandhi is shown briefly in a parody trailer for "Gandhi II" in the comedy movie UHF in which

---

207 S.Ganesh, Lage Raho Munnabhai: History as Farce, Economic and Political Review, 14-10-2006

208 Jahnu Barua, the Telegraph, Kolkata, 10-10-2006

209 Shastri Ramachandra, Jollywood Bollywood; Munnabhai rescues Mahatma, The Tribune, Chandigarh, 23-09-2006

he is described as "No more Mr. Passive Resistance". Gandhi is referred in three episodes of the sitcom Seinfeld. In the second season episode called "The Chinese Restaurant," Elaine Benes asks Jerry "Did Gandhi get this crazy?!", after George Costanza becomes verbally aggressive when beaten to a pay phone. The following season, in the episode "The Suicide", Elaine wonders aloud what Gandhi must have eaten before he fasted. Jerry responds "Oh, yeah. Gandhi loved Triscuits." The final reference to Gandhi comes in the Show's 4th season in the episode "The Old Man", when Elaine visits an old woman, Mrs. Oliver, played by Edie McClurg, who claims to have had an "affair with Mohandas." Mrs. Oliver recounts "Oh...the passion! and proceeds to show a picture of her with Gandhi to Elaine. In 'The Simpsons' episode 'Mountain of Madness' Montgomery Burns hallucinates seeing Homer Simpson conspiring against him with Mahatma Gandhi and other historical characters. Also the episode 'Homer and Apu' reveals Apu has a unique prayer said prior to eating: Good rice, good curry, good Gandhi, let's hurry. In South Park: Bigger, Longer & Uncut, during the scene where Kenny goes to hell, Gandhi is one of the ghosts seen speaking to Kenny (along with George Burns and Adolf Hitler). In Jiminy Glick in LaLaWood Jimini is seen viewing the movie "Growing up Gandhi" which depicts Gandhi as a boxer in his younger days, at the Toranto film festiville. The stop-motion animated series Robot Chicken has Gandhi saving Benjamin Franklin from the Wright Brothers in the skit "Educational Wrestling Federation" (Parody of WWE),. In a monologue, Robin Williams jokingly suggested that there should be a clothing brand called Gandhi jeans (sizes 1 and below). The Warner Bros. cartoon 'Bugs Bunny Rides Again' originally featured Yosemite Sam calling himself "The roughest, toughest, he-man stuffiest hombre as ever crossed the Rio Grande – and I don't mean Mahatma Gand-ee!" However, due to Gandhi's assassination, Mel Blanc later changed the second half of the line to "I ain't no namby-pamby!", and it has remained such ever since.[210]

Gandhi in Computer games

Gandhi has been casted in the video game series 'Civilization', as a lone leader of the Indian Civilization. He has appeared in the first three games as a lone Civilization leader, but in 'Civilization IV', he has been shown alongside Asoka. In Celebrity Deathmatch, Gandhi is casted opposite Changej Khan.

Gandhi in Music

Musicians all over the world had tried to capture the essence of Gandhi or Gandhi's idea in different forms. In India Some great classical singers had composed new Ragas on Gandhi like 'Gandhi Bilaval' by Allauddin Khan, 'Mohan Kauns' by Ravi Shankar, 'Mohan Gandhi' by Bala Murlikrishna, 'Gandhi Malhar' by Kumar Gandharva, and 'Bapu Kauns' by Amjad Ali Khan. These ragas are meant to reflect upon the personality or ideas of Gandhi in musical terms; in this way, each raga is an individual interpretation of Gandhi or Gandhism.

In west Philip Glass (b.1937) had tried to capture the essence of Gandhian Satyagraha in an opera form. It is a three act opera comprising orchestra, chorus and soloists, composed by Philip Glass, with a libretto by Glass and Constance de Jong.

---

210 http://en.wikipedia.org/wiki/List of artistic depictions of Mahatma Gandhi(accessed on 18.09.2022)

It was commissioned by the city of Rotterdam, The Netherlands, and was first performed at the Municipal Theatre there on 5th Sept.' 1980 by the Netherlands Opera and the Utrecht Symphony Orchestra, conducted by Christopher Keene. Later it was performed in UK, USA and West Germany.[211]

On the occasion of 60th death anniversary of Gandhi (January 30th, 2008) a new Dutch Musical was performed in the Amstelveen Theatre, named Gandhi. In fact the Musical was outcome of cooperation between several producers, the Gandhiserve Foundation in Berlin, the theatre of Amstelveen and Amstelveen College.

There is also some other kind of music, especially in the realm of popular music that was created all over the world, remembering Gandhi or under the influence of Gandhism like Bob Dylan: 'They Killed Him', Capitol Steps: 'The Gandhi Man', Pete Morton: Gandhi and Jesus, Silknoose: 'Gandhi Tentacle Song', Brian Spence: 'Gandhi (We will write),' 'Human: Mahatma', Manhattan Gandhi: 'Satyagraha', Patti Smith: 'Gandhi', Marti Walker: 'Compassion', Bob Livingston: 'M. Gandhi & Sitting Bull', 1001 Ways: 'Through my senses', 'Gandhi '(radio mix), Brian Boydell: 'In Memoriam Mahatma Gandhi', Barrage: 'Mahatma', Hufeisen: 'Der Tempel', Plume Latraverse: 'La Ballade De Sandale Et Gandhi', (French), Ange: 'Et Gandhi l'indoux dit tout doux,'(French), Anju Bhatt: 'Es pawan Gujarat ki dharti per'..., & others (Hindi) Mohammed

---

211 Philip Glass's style can broadly be described as minimalist, but the music in Satyagraha is somewhat more expansive than is implied by that label. The cast of the opera includes 2 sopranos, 2 mezzo-sopranos, 2 tenors, a baritone and 2 basses and a large SATB chorus. The orchestra is strings and woodwinds only, no brass or percussion.

Rafi: ;Suno suno ye Duniya Walo', (Hindi), Aufwind: 'Im Rad der Zeit', 'Harijan', 'Korrekt korrupt', 'Ahimsa', 'Gut und Böse', 'Satyagraha', 'Mantra Mahatma', (German), Howard Carpendale: 'Gandhi', (German), Bernd Stelter: 'Mahatma', (German), A Musica do oldodum: 'Mahatma Olodum', (Portuguese) and so on.

Gandhi in Painting

Gandhi is one of the most portrayed persons of 20th century although he always refused to sit or pose for artists. In his lifetime, he was mostly portrayed by his contemporary artist, like Nandlal Bose (1882–1966), Ravishankar Raval (1892–1977), Mukul Dey (1895–1989), Vinayak S. Masoji (1897–), Chaganlal Jadav (1903–1987), Kanu Desai (1907–), Feliks Topolsky (1907–1989) and Dhiren Gandhi in the period between 1918 to 1948. When he returned from South Africa, the Shantiniketan artist Mukul Dey, who was pioneer in introducing Dry points in India portrayed him in 1918 at Madras. Mukul Dey was on the trip to portray South-Indian greats, when he heard about Gandhi, who was not very known at that time in India. Mukul Dey reminisces, "My book *Twelve Portraits* had just come out at the end of 1917 and, with a view to making a collection of portraits of the great men of South India, I visited Madras in 1918. There I heard that a great leader of the

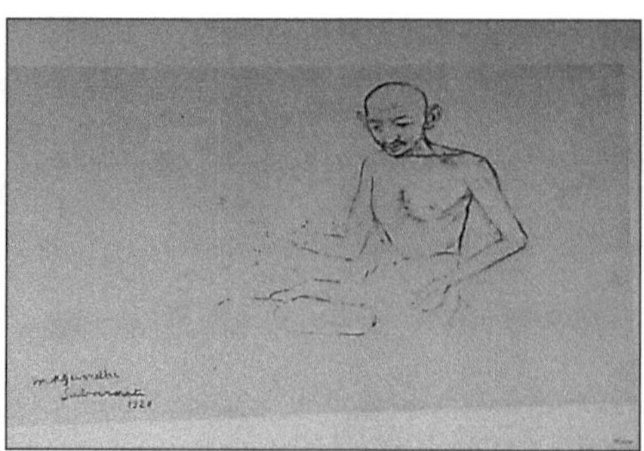

Mukul Dey: Portraits of Mahatma Gandhi (1948)

Indians of South Africa had come to stay in Madras for a few days... Mrs. Naidu then introduced me to Gandhiji and told him of my errand. Gandhiji smiled sweetly at me, as if signifying his consent to my doing his portrait. He went on talking to the people in the room, while I busied myself with my pencil. I finished the portrait within an hour. Gandhiji looked at it and said, 'Do I really look like that? Of course I cannot see my face from that angle. Then he passed it round to the persons assembled there. At my request he put down the following words in Gujrati: Mohan Das Gandhi, Phagun Badi 3, Samvat 1975."[212] In this pencil sketch Gandhi has a *shikha* (tuft of hair at the back of head) and very closely cropped hair. Two more time he portrayed Gandhi, one in 1928, at Sabarmati—four dry points and few pencil sketches and again in 1945 at Puna, where he drowned Gandhi in pencil and crayon, pen and ink. Kanu Desai is also one of the earliest artists to portray Gandhi

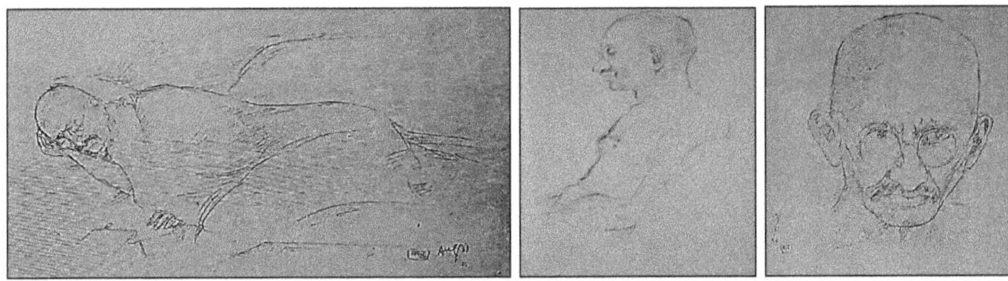

Kanu Desai: Mahatma Gandhi: Pictures in pen, pencil and Brush

that was later published with an essay by Verrier Elwin in 1932, titled "Mahatma Gandhi: Pictures in pen, pencil and Brush." Ravishankar Raval, one of the pioneers of art in Gujarat, painted Mahatma Gandhi's trial of 1922, which was held at Ahmadabad's

212 Mukul Dey, Portraits of Mahatma Gandhi, Orient Longman, 1948, preface (www.chitralekha. org)

circuit house and this painting is considered to be one of the landmark in his oeuvre. This oil painting of the court scene was based on the original pencil sketch done by him under the

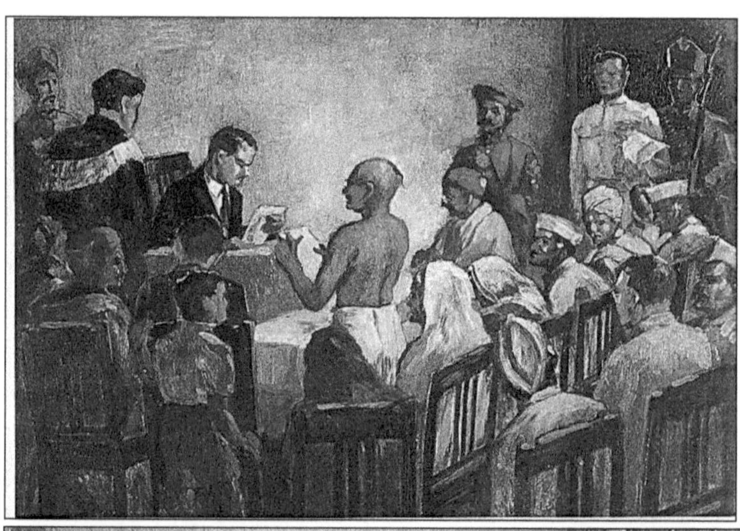

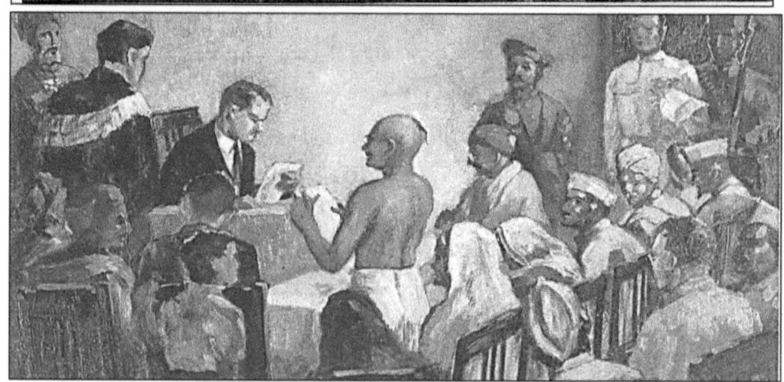

Ravishankar Raval: Hunting the Lion–
An eyewitness record of 1922 trial of Mahatma Gandhiji

very eyes of the court, so this painting has some historical authenticity attached to it. Like all other Indians Artists too were very much influenced by Gandhi and his Dandi march especially Nandlal Bose and Vinayak S. Masoji, who depicted this epic movement in all its glory. In his famous painting, "The Midnight Arrest," Masoji had compared Gandhi's arrest during his return from Dandi with the arrest of Jesus Christ at midnight in the garden of Gethsemanes. When Gandhi and Rajkumari Amrit Kaur saw this painting in the art gallery of the Congress she asked Gandhi whether the painting was based on the artist's imagination or whether it had actually happened as was depicted in the painting. Gandhi quietly and with a smile replied: "yes, yes, exactly, exactly. They came like that."[213] But the most

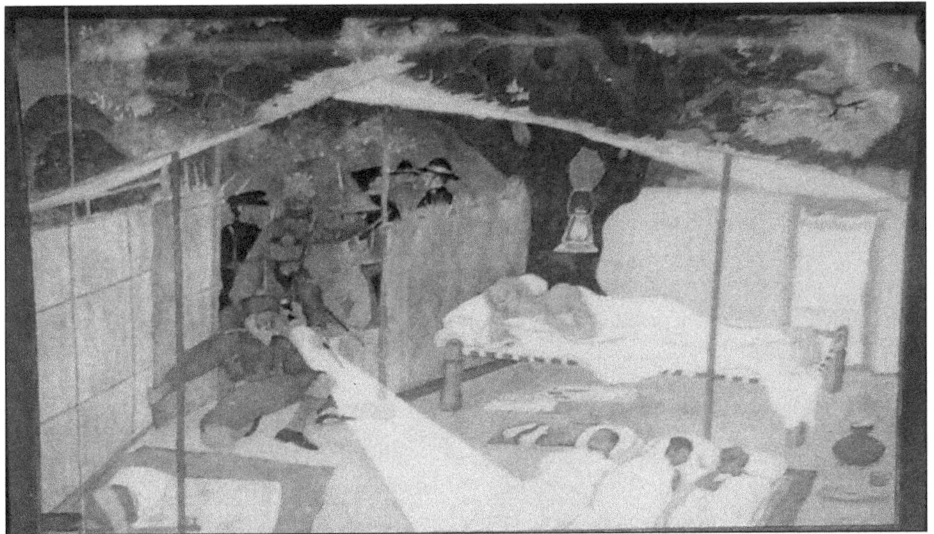

Vinayak S. Masoji, The Midnight Arrest

popular painting is Nandlal Bose's black and white linocut image of Gandhi: "Bapu Ji" made on 12th April 1930.He also made 83 panels, what is called "Haripura Posters" in patua style in the Haripura congress (1938) on Gandhi' invitation. Nandlal Bose had visualized steel mettle in a fragile looking frame

---

213 Quoted in Bhaswati Bandyopadhyay, Gandhi Marg, Volume 26, Number 3, October-December 2004

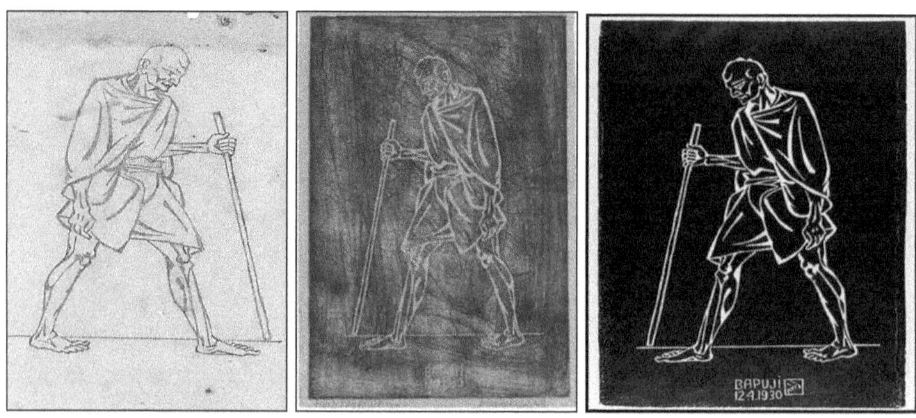

Nandalal Bose, Mahatma Gandhi walking during the protest.
29.5 × 18.2 cm. (11.6 × 7.2 in.)

of Gandhi. Dhiren Gandhi, the grand-nephew of Gandhi Ji had also portrayed him in so many sketches, that later got published

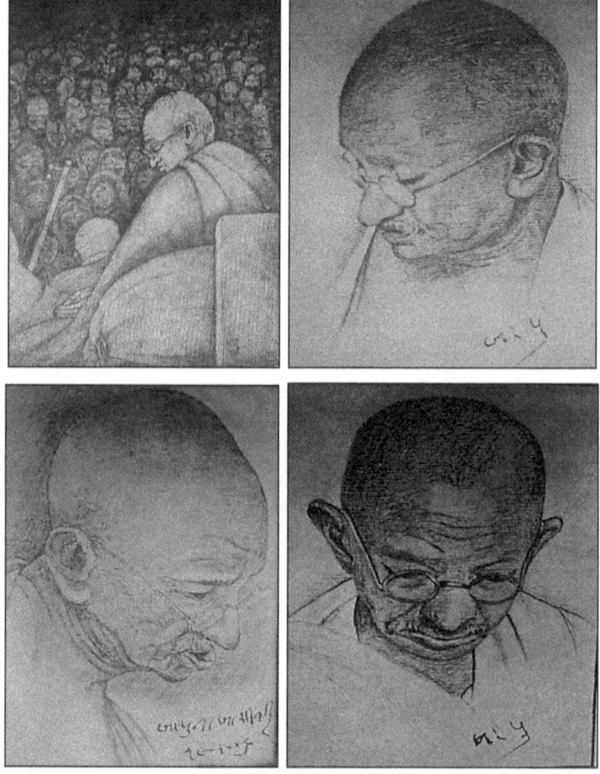

Dhiren Gandhi : Prayer and Other Sketches of Mahatma Gandhi

titled *Prayer and other Sketches of Mahatma Gandhi*.'[214] These Sketches reveal some intimate reading of the subject. When Gandhi ji went London to attend second round table conference (September 1931 – December 1931) many artists from Europe and America like Elias Mandel Grossman (1898–1947), Joe Davidson (1883–1952), Nancy Cox-McCormack (1885–1967), Clare Sheridan (1885–1970), and Clair Leighton (1898–1989) tried to capture him in

Clare Leighton, 1931 Elizabeth Brunner, 1934 Elizabeth Brunner, 1934

their respective art-forms. Clair Leighton's drawing tried to seize the historical moment of a lone leader who is struggling to convince not only his opponents but his own compatriots during second Round Table Conference. On the other hand, Hungarian artist Elizabeth Brunner (1910–2001) encounters Mahatma in relatively more relaxed environment at Kunoor, she writes, "When the portrait was finished, I handed it over to him. His face lit up with approval, and he willingly wrote his signature. The news flashed the country, 'Hungarian artist paints the Mahatma in half an hour.' He told us that we could come anytime

214 Dhiren Gandhi, Prayer and other Sketches of Mahatma Gandhi, Nalanda Publication, Mumbai, 1948.

we pleased to observe him freely through his daily routine."[215] Feliks Topolski, the Polish artist who later became British citizen visited India in 1944–46 and portrayed Gandhi through pencil, pen and brush. These paintings seem to presuppose the assassination of Gandhi and that way achieve a kind of reputation for the analysis of the premonition of artists. In Rashtrapati Bhavan, where this painting is displayed, the following information is given: [The painting]... shows Mahatma Gandhi

Felix Topolsky:Sketches in 1944

bathed in blood leaning on two young women, calmly slumping to the ground. It was painted in 1946, as if in precise premonition of Gandhi ji's assassination two years later. It was later re-worked as part of a large four-panel painting titled, *The East 1948* which Jawaharlal Nehru acquired on a visit to London in 1949." Mahatma Gandhi was assassinated on January 30, 1948. Now the question is how Topolski visualized the precise details of the assassination? There are two paintings: one done in 1946 and another a reworked version in 1948. There are some similarities and some differences in these two versions as Art historian

---

215 https://www.theheritagelab.in/elizabeth-brunner-dream-india/(accessed on 18.09.2022)

Sumathi Ramaswamy has pointed out that the "Notice the presence, in the bottom right of the canvas [in the 1946 painting],

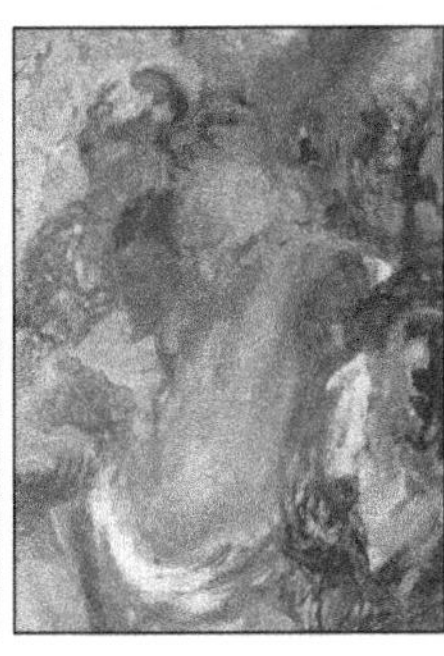

Felix Topolsky: a. The reworked painting of 1948 displayed at the Rashtrapati Bhavan, India

b. Mysterious Strokes: Topolski's 1946 painting of Gandhi

c. Mahatma Gandhi walking past

of a disembodied hand with a smoking gun pointing towards us. ...In the 1948 painting, notice a dark figure has been placed behind the gun."[216] It is true that the threat to Gandhi Ji's life since 1946 was hanging in the air but the whole atmosphere in the depiction of the subject resembles so much to what really happened later is truly baffling.

After Gandhi's assassination, Chaganlal Jadav, the great renaissance artist of Gujarat painted an abstract series of thirteen paintings as a form of mourning. His sketches of Gandhi and others during Dandi march are full of vigour and vitality. Here Gandhi appears as a man of action who even in his sleep seems making blueprints for national independence.

---

216 https://www.theweek.in/theweek/cover/2019/06/21/assassination-painting-of-gandhi-at-rashtrapati-bhavan-an-exercise-in-myth-making.html (accessed on 18.09.2022)

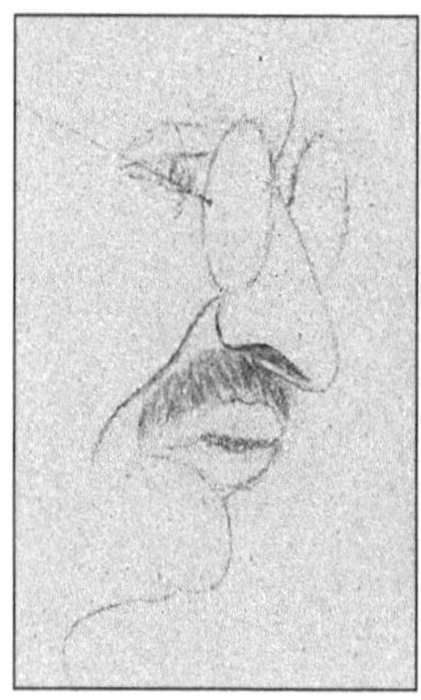

Chhaganlal Jadav,
During Dandi
March, pencil on
paper, 6.5 × 9.8 cm,
1932

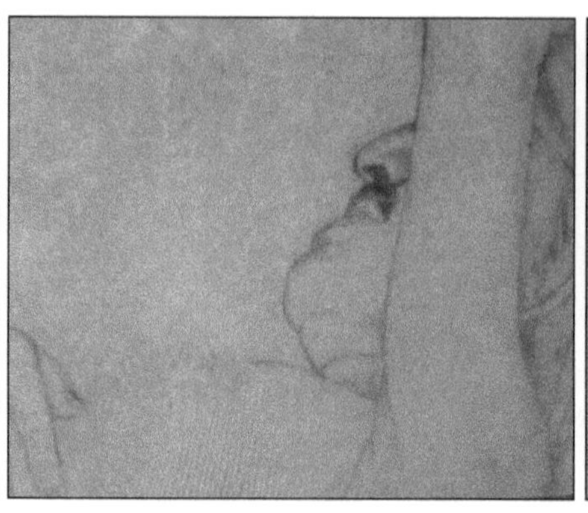

Pencil on paper, 8.6 × 12.3 cm,
RanchodlalShodhan's bungalow
(19-7-1933)

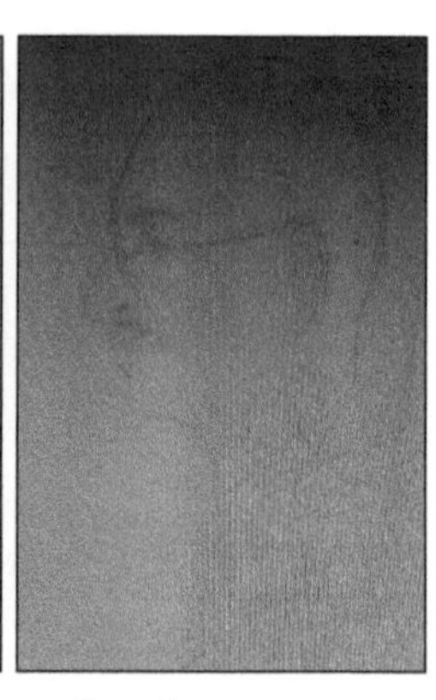

Pencil on paper,
25.×33.4 cm,
Collection:
Dr. Rizwan Kadri

Over the years, modernist artist like, K. K. Hebbar (1911–1996), M. F. Husain (1915–2011), K.G. Subramanian (1924–2016), Manu Parekh (1939–) had tried to explore some of the distinct dimensions of the personality of Gandhi. K.K. Hebbar's Gandhi seems very soothing to look at and to some extant It appears like official portrait of Gandhi, whereas Hussain presents him in his typical semi figurative cum abstract style with vibrant colours that expresses ideas and concepts regarding the man and his world. K.G. Subramanian made the mural for Gandhi Darshan, Delhi on the concept of Gandhism, while Manu Parekh over the years painted Gandhi in so many moods, so many medium and in so many ways. He was fascinated as if with the emotions as communicative skill of a mass leader can be interpreted on

K.K.Hebbar: Oil on Canvas: 22"W × 29"H M.F.Hussain: Gandhi, ca. 1970–1979, watercolor and acrylic on paper 142.2 × 85.1 cm. (56 × 33.5 in.)

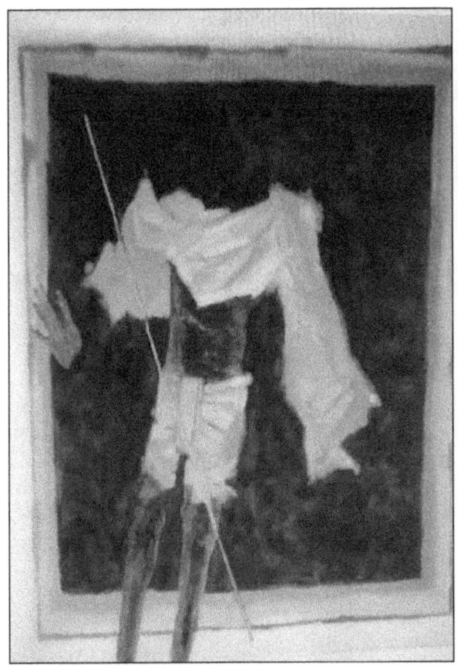 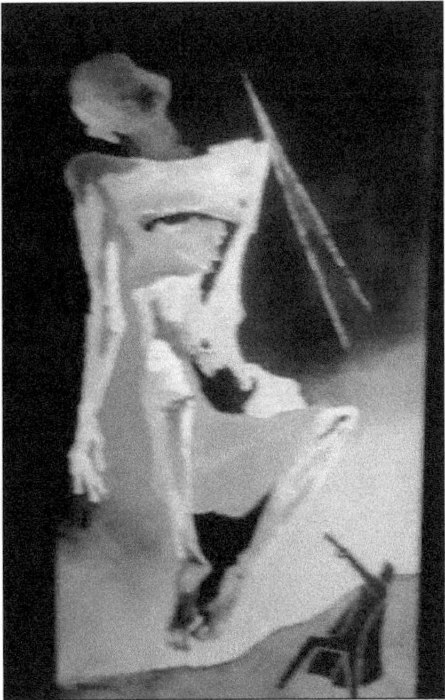

Assisination of Gandhi Acrylic on canvas, 163 × 95 cm

Manu Parekh's Gandhi

a visual plane so transparantly that it may become a kind of testimonial of history and at the same time an artistic statemet as well. He often happens to say, "When I paint a head, I'm not really painting a head, I'm painting an expression. And when I paint an expression, I'm actually painting a situation."[217] Nowhere is it truer than his Gandhi portraits.

Manu Parekh's Gandhi: 1. Oil on Board, 40 × 29.5, inch, 2004   2. Oil on canvas, 30 × 24 in., 2005   3. Oil on canvas, 48 × 48 inch, 2005

217 https://www.firstpost.com/living/manu-parekhs-canvasses-a-retrospective-spanning-60-years-of-the-artists-work-highlights-his-vitality-4098303.html (accessed on 15.09.2022)

4. Acrylic on canvas 48 × 48   5. Acrylic on canvas, 29 × 23   6. Mixed Media on Paper,
inch, 2005   inch, 2011   40 × 30 inch, 2014

Atul Dodiya (1959–) re-imagined Gandhi in a way that was characterized by Ranjit hoskote as an artist of Non-violence, he writes. "Atul's watercolours have led the Mahatma out of the tumultuous pages of history into the gentle sepia-washed terrain of his canvas. Here, Gandhi is given a new lease of life with sensitive brush strokes. A rich burnt sienna reaffirms the strength and spirit of Gandhi beneath the frail 'minimalist' body. Luminous yellow-whites merge into deep ambers inviting a closer scrutiny of nuances. Shades, we must remember that make the fabric of humanity. Shades, that Gandhi urged, we embrace as one people."[218] Atul Dodiya has been working on Gandhi since his childhood but exhibition happened in Gallery Chemould, Mumbai, 1999. In this exhibition his paintings in watercolours were far more personal and intimate then his usual oil on canvas. This show was proved revealing not only for viewers but artist

---

218 Ranjit Hoskote, "Re-imagining Bapu", An Artist of Non-violence, Gallery Chemould, Mumbai, pp.30–32

Atul Dodiya; Lamentation (1997).

Atul Dodiya: Bapu at Rene block Gallery, New York-1974, 1998

himself too found expression for his conceptual art, as Atul Dodiya cites "There are images of Gandhi everywhere. Every second street is named after him, his face is on stamps, on currency, in government offices, but his spirit is nowhere. As I reflected on him I began to realize that Gandhi had much in common with a new art technique called conceptual art. The series changed my life, and my concerns shifted to the social arena. Today, I feel Gandhi is more relevant than ever before."[219] As if to emphasize this fact the most comprehensive attempt to contemplate in modern times on Gandhi or Gandhism was an exhibition titled 'Satyagraha - Indian and South African artists' tribute to the spirit of 9-11-1906", organized by 'Afrikhadi.' in

219 https://www.saffronart.com/sitepages/articledetails.aspx?articleid=867   (accessed   on
    18.09.2022)

2006 in Delhi and Durban[220]. This show was a commemorative exhibition of the centenary of 'Satyagraha', where sixty seven artists from India and South Africa had participated.[221] Some of the exciting works of this show were K G Subramanian's "The earth is given to us in trust" in Mixed media, Gulam

Gulammohammed Sheikh, His Satyagraha and Ours, gouache on arche paper, 2006

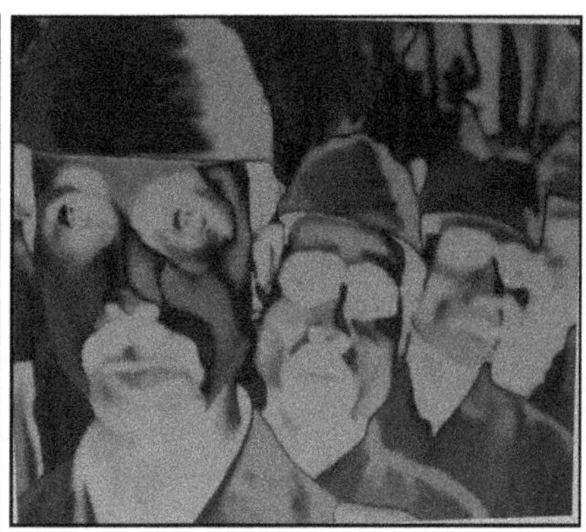

T.V. Santosh (1968), How Far is the Freedom? 2006, oil on canvas, 99.4 × 122 cm. (39 × 48 in.)

---

220 Satya Graha: Indian and South African Artists' Tribute to the Spirit of 9-11-1906 : Collection of Essays and Catalogue (ed)V. K. Cherian, Jayaram Poduval,Afrikhadi India, Kizo Gallery, Afrikhadi India and Kizo Gallery, Durban, 2006

221 Indian Artists: KG Subrahmanyan, Gulam Mohammed Sheikh, Nilima Sheikh, Vasudevan Akkitham, Indrapramit Roy, Alok Bal, Mahendra Pandya, Mayyur Kailash Gupta, Anandjit Ray, Anuj Poddar, Sumedh Rajendran, H G Arun, Soman Rajinder Tikku, Rajasekharan Nair, Karl Antao, Shatrughna Thakore, Haku Shah, Hindol Brahmabhatt, Walter D'Souza, Sudhir Patwardhan, Krishnamachari Bose, Sudarshan Shetty, Simeen Oshidar, Riyas Komu, Chintan Upadhyaya, T V Santhosh, Anup Panikkar, Suryakant Lokhande, Vivek Vilasini, Tushar Joag, Abhimanue V G, Subba Ghosh, Iranna Koumudi Patil, Sabu Joseph, Murali Cheeroth Harindran, T K Binoy Vargheese, Benitha P SunojSonia Vinod Patel, Vinod Daroz Pradeep, Dilip Tamuly, Valsan Koleri. South-African Artists: Gabisile Nkosi Lindelani Ngwenya Sfiso Kamkame Zama Dunywa Vulindlela Nyoni Sam Nhlengthwa Vanessa Berlein Philip Briel Anthony Mutheki Hildegard Ignatius Marx Lene Pienaar Simmi Dullay Paul Lawrenson Andrew Verster Andian Walsh Cling Singh Marklyn Go vender Rani Pillai

Mohammed Sheikh's "His Satyagraha and ours" in Gauche on paper, 2006 T.V. Santosh (1968–), How Far is the Freedom?, Nilima Sheikh's "Isvar (Allah tere Jahan mein......in Tempera

Haku Shah: Satya : Serigraph on handmade paper 34 × 28 Inches

serigraphs, 71 × 86 cm / 28 × 34 inch

on handmade paperboard, Haku Shah's Untitled in Oil on Canvas, Walter D'Souza's"Satyagraha", in Wood and Metal and Krishnamachari Bose's"Gaddi of Mahatma" in Wood and Cotton. T.V. Santosh (1968–), How Far is the Freedom? is inspired by a dialogue happened to took place in 1923 between Gandhi and Sri Narayana Guru, who was a revolutionary figure from Kerala. Gandhi asked him this question about how far is freedom and Narayan Guru replied that freedom was very far away; while Gandhi, referring to vitality of Indian Independence, emphasized the opposite view that freedom was very near and almost at hand.

Another important exhibition on Gandhi in recent times was 'Postcards for Gandhi' organized by SAHMAT in 1995 at Ahmedabad, Bangalore, Mumbai, Kolkata, Chennai and Delhi in which many artists including K.G.Subramanian, Gulam Muhammad Sheikh, Nilima Sheikh, Shamshad, Vivan Sundaram,

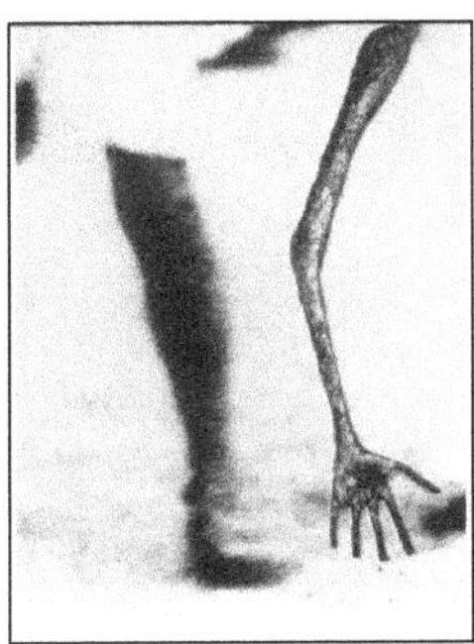

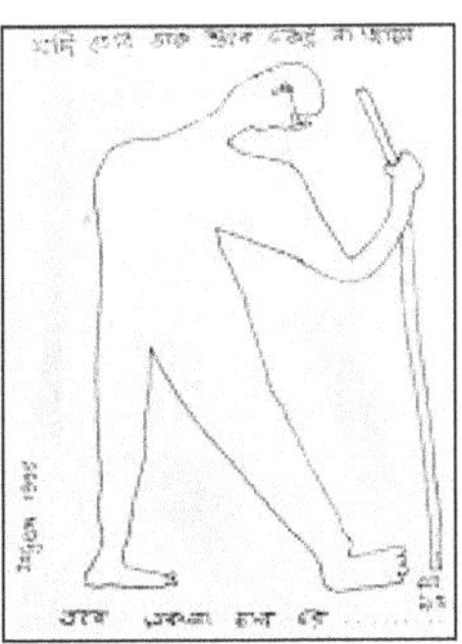

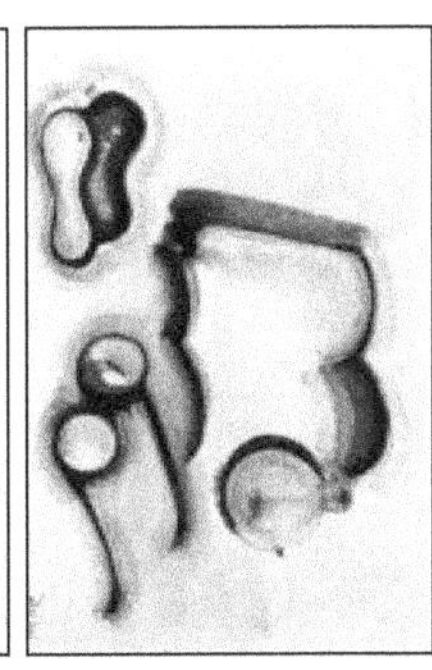

Fig. 1. K.G.Subramanian, Watercolour

2. Vivan Sundaran, collage with Photograph

3. Jogen Choudhary, ink on pastel

4. Gulammohammad Sheikh, watercolour

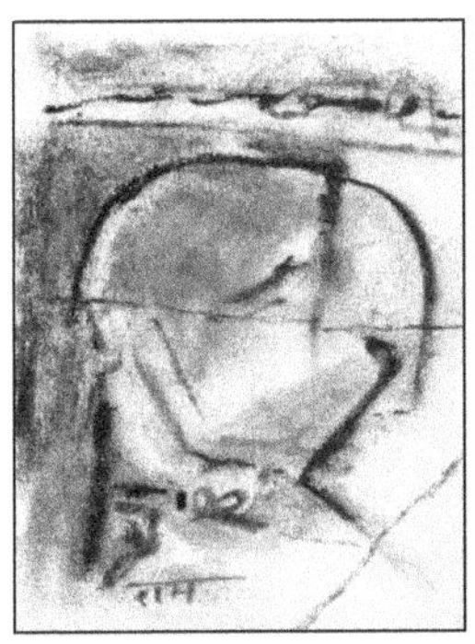

Fig 5. Ramkumar, Acquarelle

6. Vasudevan Akkitham, Conte

7. Sudhir Patwardhan, Pencil

8. Jehangir Sabavala, Mixed media

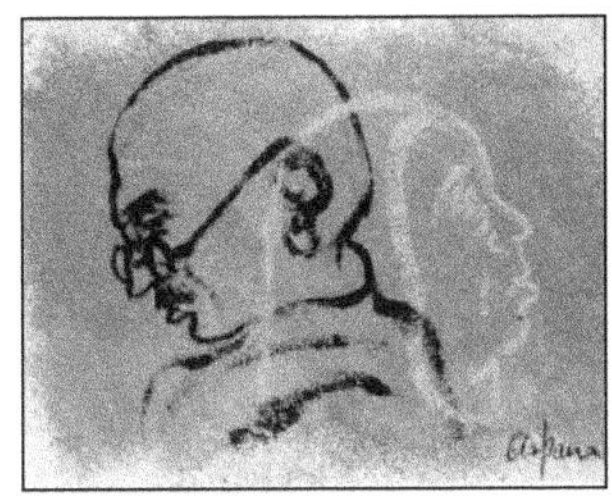

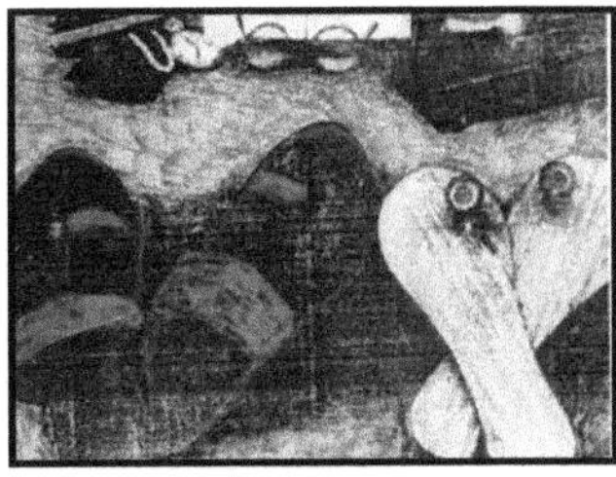

Postcards: Fig 9. Arpana Caur, Gouache

10. Rabin Mondal, ink

11. Shamshad, coloured Zerox

Jahangir Sabavala and Jogen Chowdhury, Sudhir Patwardhan were highlighted. These Postcards in their limited physical space revealed the multi-faceted genius of Gandhi in such a way that not only the inner landscape of the subject is revealed but stamp of creator is also discernable. Gandhi still continues to be the muse for many young contemporary artists that was proved again at the three-day India Art Summit in 2008 (22 to 24-08-2008). Gandhi and the environment were two themes that were most popular among younger artists. A giant spinning wheel by Smriti Arora was installed at the entrance of the Art Summit held at the Pragati Maidan, Delhi, that could be seen quite symbolically of Gandhi's strong presence in the scene of contemporary art. K. Khosa did an interesting set of paintings. A couple of years or so back, Haku Shah executed certain interesting items incorporating dry leaves and branches, khadi pieces and charkha therein, with much of a symbolic connotation. Surely the aim was to propagate the Gandhian ideals. N K Ranganath, popularly known as Ranga (1925–2002), a cartoonist, too joined the bandwagon by depicting Gandhi ji in various postures and with his lathi with great effect.

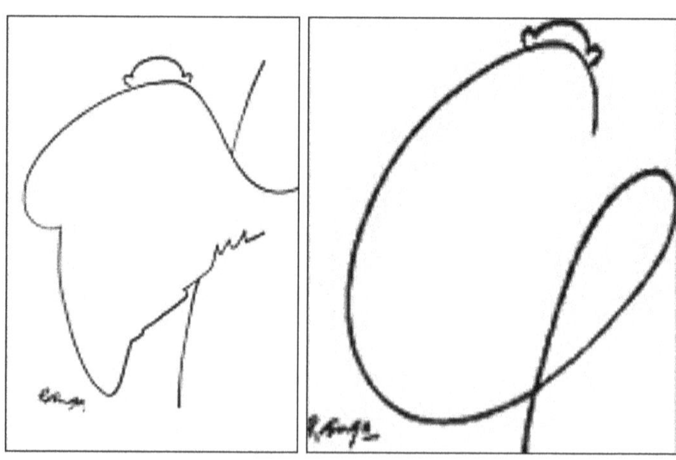

In 2019, one hundred twenty artists from all over India have come together to commemorate 150 years of Gandhi at the Lalit Kala Akademi in Delhi.[222] The show is replete with more than a 100 paintings in which Simran KS Lamba's Gandhi and Industry made with coal tar, Encaustic Wax, Metal Nuts and

Sonia Sareen, Sabarmati ke Sant, Acrylic on khadi, 2019

Washers and Jute on canvas, Vishal Joshi, The common thread, acrylic on canvas, and muralist and glass sculptor Sonia

Simran KS Lamba: Gandhi and Industry, Hemvathy Guha, the leader, woodcut, 2003

Vishal Joshi, The common thread, acrylic on canvas, 2019 42 Inches × 60 Inches

Medium: Tar, Encaustic Wax, Metal Nuts and Washers and Jute

222 https://www.architecturaldigest.in/content/mahatma-gandhiji-jayanti-artists-delhi-2019/ (accessed on 18.09.2022)

Sareen, Sabarmati ke Sant, Acrylic on khadi, 2019, Hemvathy Guha, the leader, woodcut, 2003 Vishal Joshi, The common thread, acrylic on canvas, 2019 Adwaita Gadanayak, charcoal, 1998, Jagdeesh Tammineni, The Birth Of A Nation - 1, Woodcut print on Paper, 2017 are some of the most prominent and refreshingly new. These paintings once again prove that Gandhi as a subject of an art- work is inexhaustible—generation after generation artists tried their hand and imagination to capture or explore the enigma what is called Gandhi. Tammineni, for example picks up the idea of nation building and consistently used Gandhi in his work. His series is called "Birth of a Nation."

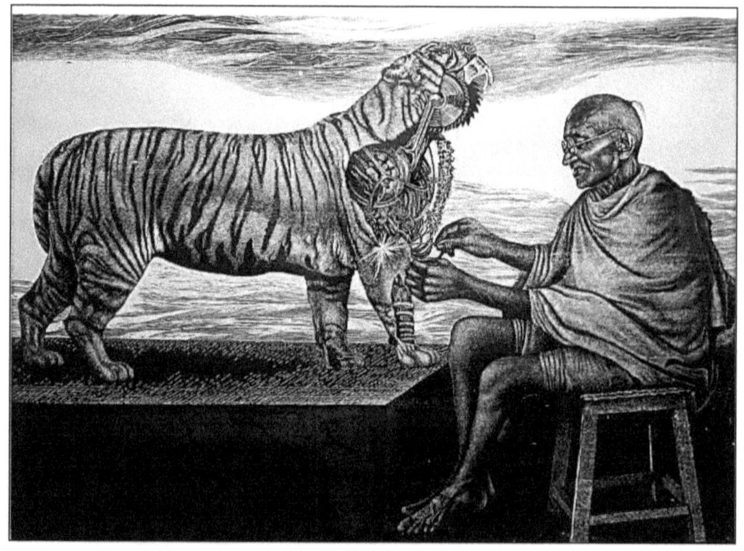

Jagdeesh Tammineni, The Birth Of A Nation - 1,
Woodcut print on Paper, 36_× 48 ins, 2017

He states, "I believe Gandhi was someone who could hold the nation/country together without it falling apart. I believe his ideas of non-violence as well as nation building are still valid in the 21st century, wrecked as we are by sectarian violence. The act of building a democratic, liberal nation has its own pitfalls and the path is strewn with difficulties. Gandhi ji still holds the key."[223] In this work Gandhi is conceived as a playful operator who may fix the mechanized machine bones of a tiger to work and function but uncanny expression of his face also reveals that he is aware of its futility and absolute absurdity of his action but he tries to interact and have dialogue with it. Similarly Subrat Kumar Behera, Adwaita Gadanayak and Paresh Maity (1965–) interpreted Gandhi in their own personal way, where artist vision of his subject is overwhelmingly intense and symbolical. Subrat tried to capture what historian Shahid Amin called 'Powers' of Mahatma Gandhi [224] in a most dramatic manner whereas Adwaita Gadanayak's meditating Gandhi, engrossed in

Subrat Kumar Behera, Gandhi,
Lithography and hand colour on paper,
19 × 24.5 inches, 2019

Adwaita Gadanayak, charcoal, 1998

223 https://www.thehindu.com/entertainment/art/mahatma-and-his-message/   article
27209365. ece (accessed on 18.09.2022)

224 See, Shahid Amin, Gandhi as Mahatma: Gorakhpur District, Eastern UP 1921–22,in Ranjit Guha (ed), Subaltern Studies III, Oxford University Press, Delhi, 1984

some deep thought is minimalist in its appearance but its impact on viewer is very moving and thought –provoking. Same is the case with Paresh Maity, who has depicted Gandhi again and again in a manner that is traditional to its core but innovative in its impact. In his tribute to Gandhi's Dandi march he tried to evoke the texture of salt and sea in mixed media as he explained, "I have mixed water colour, oil, acrylic, saw dust, different kinds of glues and all kinds of medium and to add to the effect, salt mounds are placed in front of the work at Art .The installation is an extension of the visual impression left by the artwork."[225] In another work he focused not on Gandhi but Gandhism as he himself pointed out at the time of its exhibition: "My installation, titled, "The Wheels That Spin Infinity," using khadi (denoting our freedom struggle), paper (connecting one to nature) and Origami (paper folding) expounds three ideas of the Mahatma. One is his emphasis on Gram Swaraj. The second work has 17 modules, the number of times he undertook fasting.

Paresh Maity, Swadeshi, 6.5ft-×-13ft-Oil-Acrylic-Saw-Dust-Threads-on-Canvas, 2018

---

225 https://www.telegraphindia.com/culture/arts/paresh-maity-painter-of-longest-work-pays-tribute-to-tallest-leader-gandhi/cid/1672816 (accessed on 14.09.2022)

This is to stress upon the need to cut down on excesses, renunciation and strike a balance between ecology and self. The third idea focuses on self-reliance. The 17 contemporary charkhas reflect infinity, a concept on which India and its people must work just as they did in the past to discover zero. This is my first work solely dedicated to Gandhiji's ideas."[226] Another senior artist S H Raza (1922–2016) has dedicated his last few years to paint Gandhi ji's major idea of Satya, Ahimsa, Sanmati etc.in 2013, but it was displayed as Gandhi in Raza, one year after his death in 2017 as a kind of Artist's tribute to the Mahatma and his philosophy. It was a series of seven paintings that was created to visualize some basic tenets of Gandhian philosophy such as peace, truth, compassion, goodness etc. In the medium of acrylics on canvas, artist in his long practiced motifs and colour-scheme tried to capture the essence of a man whose life was his message. It was like capturing the essence of a poem where abstraction plays the role of a concrete structure and solid melts into thin air.

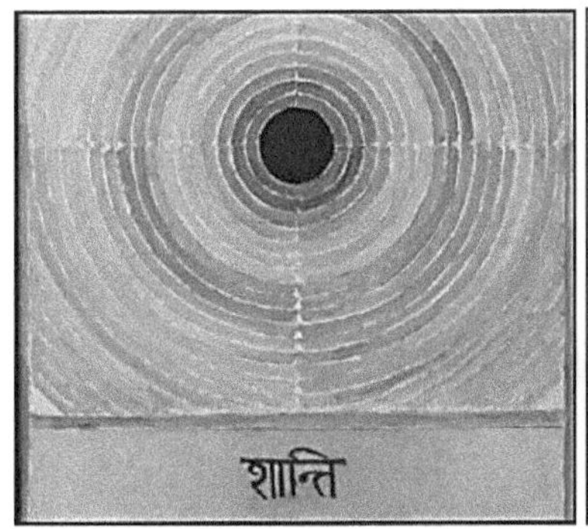

S.H. Raza: Shanti, Acrylic on canvas, 59" × 47"	Sanmati, Acrylic on canvas, 59"× 59"	Satya, Acrylic on canvas, 59" × 47"

---

226 https://www.thehindu.com/entertainment/art/many-moods-of-the-mahatma/ article29519808.ece (accessed on 14.09.2022)

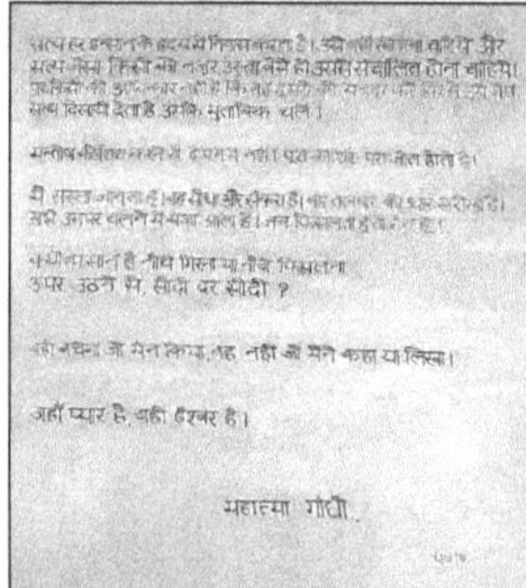

Some ideas of Gandhi, Acrylic on canvas, 59" × 47

Peed Parai, Acrylic on canvas, 59" × 59" 2013

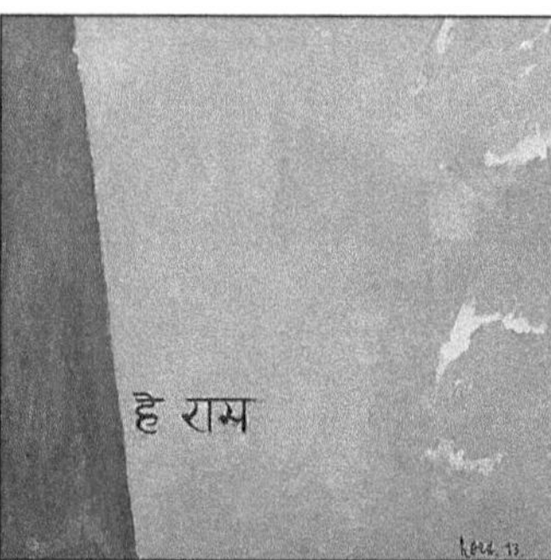

Hey Ram, Acrylic on canvas, 23.5" × 23.5

Death of Gandhi was depicted by so many artists but Tom Vattakuzhy, work (2019) is a unique creation that creates history painting in most subtle way —here a crucial moment of a rare life touches the innermost feelings of whole of a nation that is real at the same time most dramatic in its appearance. For painter it was a moment that should be reaffirmed again and again in our time as he pointed out that, "When our history is at stake, we have to reaffirm it through art. At a time when the ideologies and death of Gandhi are misinterpreted, we have to assert it through the visual language. Gandhi is more than a sentiment for us. His values have played a key role in forming our perspective. To envision an India without Gandhi is difficult for me. He is dear to us. His story and thoughts should shine bright."[227]Art critic Uma Nair opines that, "Art history states that Michelangelo had long been praised for marrying Renaissance ideals of classical beauty with poses that favoured naturalism. Another nod to Renaissance influence is the mood created by Vattakuzhy. The intense horror and grief writ large on their faces each image is a pathos filled expression. Vattakuzhy connects Gandhi to Jesus

---

227 https://timesofindia.indiatimes.com/blogs/plumage/tom-vattakuzhys-death-of-gandhi/ (accessed on 18.09.2022)

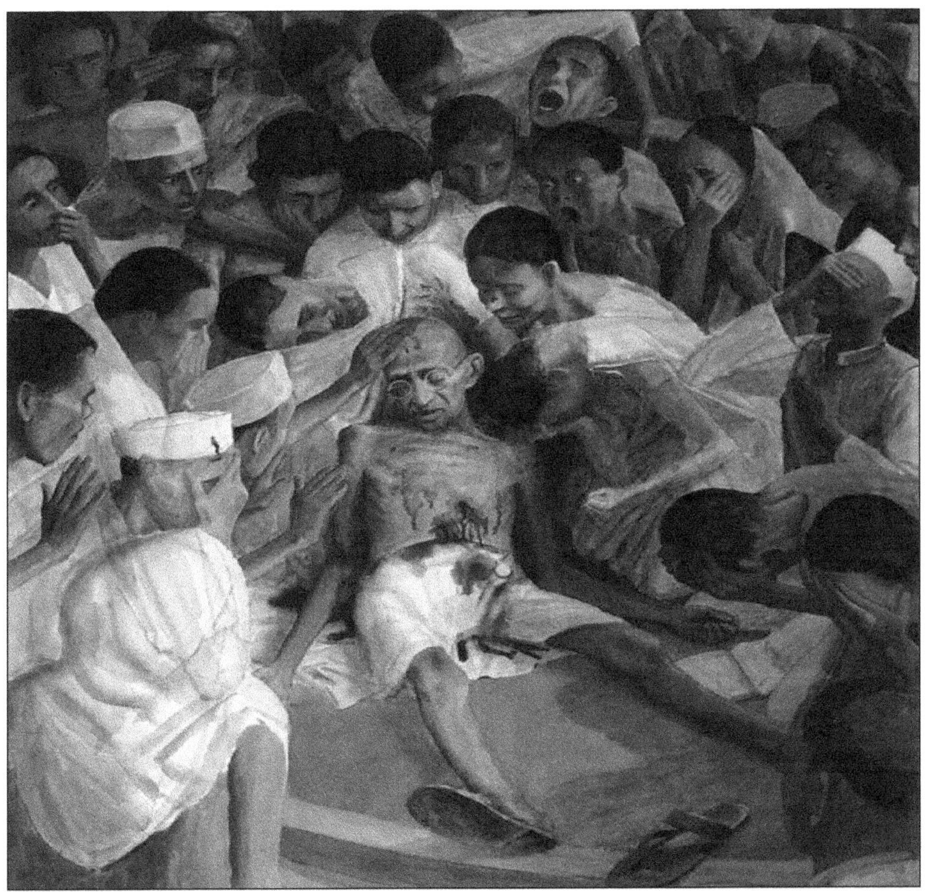

Tom Vattakuzhy, Death of Gandhi, Gouache on canson paper, 2019; https://kochipost.
com/?p=15540

Christ and his last moments after crucifixion. He considers the artist a creator of originality and feels sometimes even in the most tragic circumstances the politics of hope and hopelessness both see the light of day.

"Vattakuzhy creates a highly emotional story with the combination of elements of emotion, we also see the dimensional layout and iconography, of the expression on the faces of Manu Behen and Abha Behen, showing an emotional response to the death of Gandhi. This handling of the emotive evocation actually draws the viewer into the scene by inviting us to witness the pain and anguish of the lamentation of the death of the Mahatma. You can almost hear the silent sobs of the women and the despair of anguish from the men around sitting in disbelief. Vattakuzhy creates a realistic depiction of emotion on the human faces-turning Gandhi and everyone around into subjects of the scene of death."[228] It is true that we once again like the onlooker, witness the pain and anguish and deliverance and indulgence with unspeakable intensity.

Over the years, Gandhi has been very popular among the artists in India and it is almost impossible to document or take note of all the works in a single paper; especially when every single day some artist somewhere is painting Gandhi so at best it can be selective and consequently subjective. In recent times new generation rediscovered Gandhi in a very different context, for

| Love distributor, Charcoal and acrylic on linen 45" × 60" | Love Messenger, Charcoal and acrylic on linen, 37 × 48 inches, 2018 | Charcoal, gold leaf & acrylic on linen 39" × 57" |

example Gurmeet Marwa (b.1984) painted Gandhi in such unusual settings that the whole scenario becomes satirical in tone. His medium like charcoal, acrylic, oil, watercolours, lithograph, etching, linocut and woodcut with contrasting

---

228 ibid

colour-schemes like black with red makes the central idea more salient and sometimes more melodramatic.

Mixed Medium on canvas, 36 × 48 inches, Gandhi with a golden kart, Charcoal

Endless Journey, Charcoal and acrylic on linen

acrylic & gold leaf on linen, 48 × 50 inches, 2020 48" × 38"

Love Distributer 2 Gandhi with gang, woodcut, 22 × 33 inch

Mix Media On Canvas, 38 × 41 in, 2017

Acrylic and charcoal on linen 38" × 30"

Gandhi, not only as political thinker or mass leader or as one of the mover and shakers of twentieth century but as subject for art too he is simply inexhaustible!

Gandhi in Sculpture

The American sculptress, Nancy Cox-McCormack Cushman (1885–1967)[229] who came for 'modeling from life the portrait bust

---

229 http://www.nancyweyant.com/index.php/pages/Nancy-Cox-McCormack.html(accessed on 18.09.2022)

of Mahatma Gandhi' at the time of Round Table Conference (1931) in London writes, "Modeling a portrait is the science of building up a balanced structure into exact masses, the surface planes of which must be reconciled to convey the likeness and spirit of the subject's character. In a portrait bust there are no "voids" unless one happens to be attempting to model the head of a purposeless idiot.All the legitimate conditions being denied me I planned a bust small enough to be manageable on a turning stand, concluding that the physical proportions and a likeness imbued with the power behind Gandhi's mind would, if could get them, serve as my interpretation. It should be sculpturesque, that is a *sculpture* and not surface photography. It must be the basic Gandhi which in

Nancy Cox-McCormack: 1. Bronze bust   2. "Unfinished" signed work, given to Devdas Gandhi in London, Oct 1931

his case seemed to me to be a mobile stubbornness born of the Asiatic Hindu philosophy...I do not mind admitting that besides all that I was delving for the substance of the Mahatma's personal panorama as a Hindu Holy Man and as politician."[230] It is obvious that Sculptress is absolutely clear about the substance of her subject Gandhi, that is Hindu Holy man and politician then nothing remains for interpretation but if we see the sculpture and consider the historical circumstances in which subject Gandhi was in, it was the one of the most trying time of his whole political life and consequently the frustration and sense of defeat that is very much evident in her sculpture too needs some exploration. Is it not an example of Art transcending the Artist?

When she was packing up after three weeks session with Gandhi in Kingsley Hall, London, another compatriot of her, the well-known sculptor Joe Davidson (1883–1952), Commissioned by associated press took her space there to complete his assignment. He commented about his subject's profile in his Memoir: "Gandhi's face was very mobile, every feature quivered, and a constant change played over his face when he talked. He practiced his passive resistance on me all the time while I worked; he submitted to my modeling him, but never willingly lent himself to it. Never once did he look at the clay I was working on. But when I stopped for a breather and just sat with him, he was extremely amiable."[231]No wonder his bronze sculpture reveals amiability of Gandhi in the way his slightly open eyes and mouth were depicted and that was

---

230 Nancy Cox-McCormack Cushman, Five Weeks in London, England 1931: Modeling From Life the Portrait Bust of Mahatma Gandhi, Tennessee Historical Quarterly, Vol. 19, No. 2, June, 1960, p. 152

231 See, Jo Davidson, Between Sittings: An Informal Autobiography of Jo Davidson, The Dial Press, New York, 1951

Jo Davidson, Bronze,
H 48.3 cm, W 57.cm

D 31. 1931 Clare Sheridan,
Bronze, 4.5 feet, 1932

Józef Goslawsky,
Bronze, 1932

supplemented by highlighting his shaven head and wrapped chaddar around his shoulders. But It is on record that later in life when Gandhi Ji came to know that his statue was proposed to be installed in an forthcoming session of the Congress, he dissented in Harijan on February 11, 1939 by saying: "It will be a waste of good money to spend Rs. 25,000 on erecting a clay or metallic statue of the figure of man who is himself made of clay..."[232] Despite his indifference, he was amiable towards sculptors all through his life and allowed them to 'do their business' while he is working. Other than Nancy Cox-McCormack (1885–1967) and Joe Davidson, British Clare Sheridan (1885–1970) and Dutch Clara Quien (1903–1987), also got the opportunity to meet and sculpt Gandhi. Józef Goslawsky (1908–1963), the polish sculptor and designer of medals and coins made a caricature sculptor of Gandhi too in 1932 but it was cast in bronze in 2007.

Clare Sheridan, famous sculptress of Vladimir Lenin, Leon Trotsky, Felix Dzerzhinsky and Kamenev, a cousin of Winston Churchill and once beloved of Charlie Chaplin reminisces

---

232 https://epaper.telegraphindia.com/calcutta/2018-10-21/71/Page-12.html   (accessed   on   18.09.2022)

Clare Sheridan, Bronze, close-up

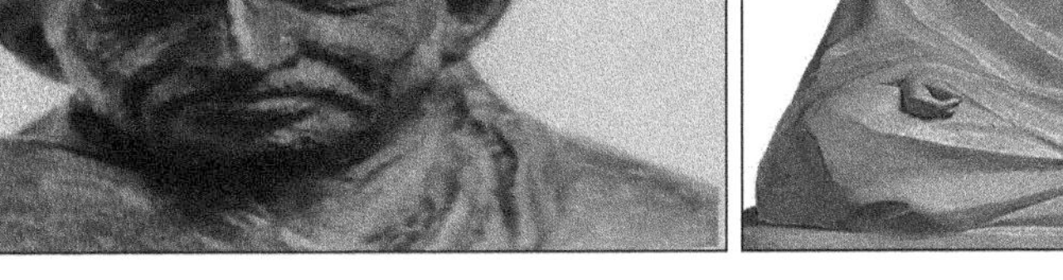

Clare Sheridan, Terracotta, 18 7/8 × 16 1/8 in (48 × 41 cm), 1934

Gandhi in these words: "I was privileged to see him "close-up" during those round table conference days; through my friend Sarojini Naidu the mahatma was induced to allow me to model his portrait...It was not easy. He would not pose. This was either by modesty, through overwork, or because he was not interested in Art! Probably all three...I had an opportunity of comparing notes with the American Sculptor, Joe Davidson who also modelled a head of Gandhi. Joe Davidson has modelled most of the prominent men of our time, and we agree they were disappointing to meet. Hardly one of them would leave an impression if he had not been "dished up" with recognizable trimmings of sentries and a background of usurped palaces. But Gandhi Stands out above all these. In his grandiose simplicity the little bare-legged man, wrapped around in his "Khaddar" is deeply impressive."[233] She sculpted him in bronze And terracotta—thoroughly meditative and inward looking, these closed eyes of Gandhi open up to a different world altogether where you happen to meet your real self. It is no coincidence that these sculptures of Gandhi,

233 Clare Sheridan, The Great Little Mahatma in S. Radhakrishnan (ed.), Mahatma Gandhi: Essays and Reflections, George Allen & Unwin Ltd., London, Second (enlarged) edition, 1949, p 273.

especially terracotta one reminds us Buddha —the same tranquility and the same composer of a great personality as she aptly describes: "A statuette of him, in the cross-legged position in which he sat weaving, has the place of honour on my writing table. Actually he looking down intent upon his weaving, but to me he is a Buddha in deep contemplation, and I sense the flow of cosmic thoughts that emanate from his memorable quietude."[234]And it may be added here that the same flow of cosmic thoughts emanate from her sculpture too and by any means it is no mean achievement. Clara Quien (1903–1987), a Dutch -British sculptress created the life-size statue of Gandhi in clay at Sewagram, Wardha *live* and later it was cast in bronze.

Clara Quien, Gandhi in terracotta, 1946   Clara Quien, Gandhi in Bronze

The essence of Gandhi and his philosophy was apprehended in most authentic way in India by two sculptors—Devi Prasad Roy Chowdhury (1899–1975) and Ram V. Sutar (1925–). Devi Prasad Roy Chowdhury has written epic poetry in stone by sculpting Dandi March in its full glory. Ten persons following Gandhi create such an energy and action that you feel like

---

234 Ibid 275

marching in a mass movement for something noble and just. And you can almost feel the vive of Gandhi and his aura. It is one of the great sculptures of modern India. It is installed on the T-junction of the Sardar Patel Marg, New Delhi. Roychoudhary's Gandhi marching to Dandi is also installed in Marina beach, Chennai. Standing on a 12-ft-highpedestal, the black bronze statue is a milestone in the history of modern sculpture in

Dandi March, Deviprasad Roychaudhury, 26-m-long and 3-m-high bronze

Deviprasad Roychaudhury,
Marina Beach, Chennai.

Ram Vanji Sutar, Indian Parliament,
New Delhi 16-feet high, bronze

India. But the most sought after statue of Gandhi all over India and the world is Ram Vanji Sutar's (1925–), who has created more than 370 sculptures of Gandhi in duration of more than 60 years and among them installed at Sansad Bhavan is the most iconic.[235]. Uma Nair writes, "Sutar's Gandhi is a large seated figure at the Indian Parliament. His decision to portray Gandhi as a gravity filled persona in seated somberness marks a radical departure from traditional representations of the guise of an old man. His lack of conventional accessories makes Gandhi's identity articulate and aesthetic in a tranquil way, opening up the possibility that Gandhi can be both real as well as allegorical as a figure head."[236] After all like any art-form sculpture is also an outcome of artist's perception of the subject, Sutar elaborates: "His shoulders were important, so was the drape of the cloth that fell from his shoulders, as well as his hands. I was creating a posture for an apostle of peace. His notion of peace was based on non-violence and forgiveness."[237] And it is true that what artist has tried to achieve in his creation, fully succeeded in its execution. No wonder this bust of Mahatma Gandhi is very popular worldwide and copies of it have been presented by the Govt. of India to foreign countries on the occasion of Gandhi Centenary Celebrations. According to Anil Sutar, son of the sculptor, "The Indian Council for Cultural Relations, which wanted to present Gandhi statues to foreign governments to commemorate the Mahatma's birth centenary, called 15 artists

---

235 https://timesofindia.indiatimes.com/blogs/plumage/ram-sutar-and-mahatma-gandhi-the-journey-goes-back-to-many-decades/(accessed on 18.09.2022)

236 ibid

237 https://www.thehindu.com/entertainment/art/many-moods-of-the-mahatma/article29519808.ece(accessed on 18.09.2022)

Ram Vanji Sutar: Gandhi in Bronze displaying different moods

to send in models of their work. The Council sent pictures to various countries, asking them to make their choices. All the countries signed on the picture of my father's model. Since then Gandhi statues made by my father have been installed in more than 200 cities across the world."[238] The popularity of this particular sculpture lies in its ability to invite onlookers for deeper observation and understanding. Tejinder Singh Baoni opines, "In Ram Sutar's work you can see he brings in the real inner character of Gandhi the whole burden, his whole responsibility and the dignified meditation."[239] It is also true as art historian and sculptor Deepak Kannal rightly pointed out that "Even when Gandhiji smiled, there was a streak, an undercurrent of pathos...I think Ram Sutar is the only person who can capture that pathos."[240] No wonder, perhaps for this exquisite quality, this Bronze busts of Mahatma Gandhi were sent to so many countries like Germany, Australia, Italy, USA, Morocco, Mexico, South Africa, Peru, Seychelles, United

238 https://scroll.in/article/674358/two-indian-sculptors-have-created-most-of-the-gandhi-statues-around-the-world(accessed on 18.09.2022)
239 ibid
240 ibid

Kingdom, Chile, Trinidad and Tobago, Canada, Ivory Coast, Fiji, Myanmar, Ecuador, Tajikistan, Russia, Syria, Brazil, Djibouti, Senegal, Martinique, Colombia, France, Argentina, Kazakhstan, Belgium, Cyprus, Serbia and Montenegro and Ethiopia.[241]A similar double heroic size bust made for International Trade Fair Asia '72 is erected as a permanent feature at Pragati Maidan in Delhi. An another monumental statue (13 feet) of Mahatma with two underprivileged children, that is erected in sandur, Bangalore, Delhi Public School, Noida and Gandhi Smriti, Delhi shows prowess and dexterity of his hands. The same theme repeated in a statue installed at St. Xavier High school, Patna. This 72 feet high bronze statue is the tallest statue of Gandhi ever made. In this statue Gandhi is seen standing affectionately with two children on either side and in the pedestal some inscriptions and images of Champaran Satyagraha in 1917, Dandi March in 1930, Quit India Movement in 1942 are depicted. Some memorable quotes of Gandhi have also been inscribed on the plaques. Sculptor himself explained it in these words:, "In 1995, I made Gandhi with the two children for the Bihar government. Since he always spoke against caste discrimination, I created the sculpture to show compassion and deep love. I wanted that spirit of togetherness to be seen by the people who look at it from afar. I wanted to include an element of his philosophy, so at the bottom of the sculpture I added, 'Mera jeevan mera sandesh hai' (my life is my message)."[242]

---

241 https://www.oneindia.com/2010/11/30/mahatmagandhi-statues-and-busts-popularworldwide.html(accessed on 18.09.2022)

242 ibid

Ram Vanji Sutar: Gandhi Smriti   St. Xavier High school, Patna
(Birla Bhavan)

Ramkinkar Baij (1906–1980) sculpted Gandhi in 1948 just after his assassination in typical expressionist and semi-expressionist form. His eight bronze statues of Gandhi walking in fast pace are stylized to various degrees that is generally recognized as Dandi march, even National Gallery of Modern Art, New Delhi where at present it is housed, refers it as Dandi March but as Siva Kumar says it actually refers to the heroic efforts of Gandhi at Noakhali, it shows him walking across the killing fields of communalism, crushing death under his feet so to speak .The skull beneath Gandhi's feet and the legend 'the Apostle of Non-violence' inscribed on the pedestal certainly points to such an idea."[243] In these statues, it is clear that sculptor is not interested

---

243 https://m.facebook.com/439885819479987/photos/a.518871624914739/1088951051240124/?t
    ype=3&_se_imp=1lYAWdGryZ6uxV03j (accessed on 18.09.2022)

in capturing the likeness of his subject rather he wants to interpret him with his own ideas and for that matter if he has to deform it, no issue for him at all. Siva Kumar has rightly pointed out that, "Evidently, it was not Ramkinkar's intention to do a conventional portrait of Gandhi; he wanted to create a figure embodying his vision of Gandhi, a vision in which Gandhi was a

Ramkinkar Baij: Dandi March or Noakhali March? Executed in 1948, cast in 1972; from an edition of eight Bronze, 18 .3/4 x 9. 1/2 x 11. 1/2 in.

metaphor for human energy - a man 'who appeared to be sprinting when he walked'... With the head lowered, his Gandhi... is immersed in thought even as he strides ahead. It is... an attempt to give a formal and somewhat abstract expression to it. In it the body is geometrized and construed as intersecting forces rising spirally upwards From the base. This is noticeable more clearly when the sculpture is viewed in the round and the spiral development of the form, and the forward movement of the figure is experienced as counterpoised within in its dynamic rhythm."[244]

---

244 R. Siva Kumar, Ramkinkar Baij: A Retrospective, 1906–1980, Delhi Art Gallery and the National Gallery of Modern Art, New Delhi, 2012, p.262

Ramkinkar Baij: cement & stone,
Kalabhavan, Shantiniketan, 1968

Ramkinkar Baij: Bronze, 18 feet, high,
1972, Guwahati

Ramkinkar Baij sculpted Gandhi again for Shantiniketan in 1968, that is a concrete structure made of cement and stone, making somehow more conventional where likeness was maintained but some kind of symbolism was introduced by depicting human skulls under Gandhi's foot. The statue depicts Gandhi with a lathi on one hand and a batuwa in another. His facial expressions are portrayed extremely disenchanted. The tragedy of partition and failure of his long cherished philosophy of non-violence took a tall on his last few months of his life and sculptor tried to capture that disenchantment in most undramatic way. This statue was casted in bronze-later and installed in Guwahati in 1972. The cement statue is still in Shantiniketan.

 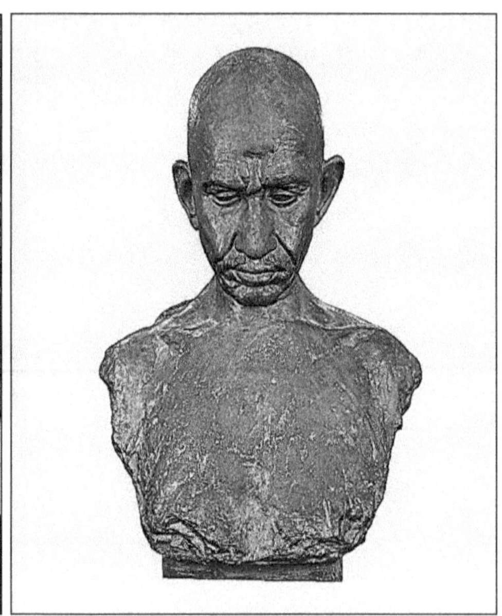

Vinayak Pandurang Karmarkar, Gandhi, Bronze, Nairobi, 1956 Gandhi Bust, Bronze, Mani Bhavan, Mumbai, 1925

With the rise of Gandhian philosophy and recognition of this great soul evoked so many commemorative statue being installed in so many distant countries. Vinayak Pandurang Karmakar (1891–1967)'s Bronze sculpture was installed at Nairobi in 1956, that was unveiled by then vice-president S. Radhakrishnan. Karmakar was one of the early artists who sculpted Gandhi ji *live* in early days of his political life in India. His work on Gandhi, especially bust is raw and unassuming in his appearance but evokes innocence and purity. Sadashiv Sathe (1926–2021) is famous for his 5-metre high statue of Mahatma Gandhi installed at National Salt Satyagraha Memorial, Dandi, Navsari but in the year 1952, he sculpted Gandhi bust in Bronze, that is remarkable for its simplicity

Sadashiv Sathe, Bronze, 1952   S.G.Srikhande, Hey Ram, Bronze

and articulation. The same way bronze bust titled *Hey Ram* by S.G Srikhande (1934–) is simply expressive of innermost state of the subject as art connoisseur Ritu Sharma opines "With his closed eyes, calmness prevails on his face which stands in communion with the significant representation of three monkeys in a garlanded *manner encircling his neck.*"[245]

In Latin American countries Gandhi statues were installed in Rio de Janeiro (Sankho Chaudhary), Sao Paulo (Biman Bihari Das) and Londrina (Gautam Pal). Busts of Mahatma Gandhi sculpted by Biman Bihari Das (1943–) were also installed in Venezuela, Spain and Italy. In Argentina, Adolfo Pérez Esquivel (1931–) the well-known human right activist and noble laureate paid his tribute by sculpting Gandhi that was installed in Gandhi Square,

---

245 https://www.devdiscourse.com/article/arts/211974-mahatma-gandhis-sculpture-features-in-exhibition-at-national-gallery-of-modern-art(accessed on 18.09.2022)

Sankho Chaudhuri, Rio de Janeiro, 1969

Biman Bihari Das

Sao Paulo Adolfo Pérez Esquivel, Barcelona, 2000

Barcelona in 2000. Belgian artist Rene Cliquet (1899–1977) sculpted in bronze one of the oldest statues of Mahatma Gandhi in Europe. The statue was installed in 1969 At Park Marie Josee in the Commune of Molenbeek, Brussels to mark the 100th

Rene Cliquet, Bronze, Brussels, 1969

Ramesh Bisht, Bronze, Netherlands

Birth Anniversary of Gandhi. This was the occasion when Gandhi statues were installed in most of the countries. Polish sculptress Fredda Brilliant (1903 –1999) Sculpted Gandhi on this

Fredda Brilliant, NGMA, New Delhi, Bronze model, Acc. No. 3392 Tavistock Square, London, 1969

Portland stone & Bronze, H 119 × W 110 × D 100 cm (E); Plinth: H 188 × W 122 × D 116 cm (E)

occassion and it was installed at Tavistock Square, London in 1969. Another statue sculpted by Phillip Jackson was installed at Parliament square, London in 2015. It was dedicated as a commemoration of the centenary of Gandhi's return to India from South Africa that is considered to be the beginning of 'Gandhi Age' in India.

Phillip Jackson, Gandhi and Close up view of the statue

London's Parliament Square. 9 feet tall, bronze, 2015

The several statues of Mahatma Gandhi in different cities of the United States are installed; Prominent among these are Union Square, New York, Martin Luther King, Jr. Center and Martin Luther King, Jr. International Chapel in Atlanta, Mahatma Gandhi Center in Houston, San Francisco Ferry Terminal, International Peace Park, Salt Lake City and Mahatma Gandhi Center, St. Louis. In 2000, one particular standing statue, which was installed in Washington D.C., is very remarkable. Sculpted by Gautam Paul (1949–) This bronze statue (8 feet 8 inches excluding pedestal of 9'×7'×3'4".) shows Dandi march and the many padyatras he undertook throughout the length and breadth of the Indian sub-continent. In America people like Bob Clyatt, Joseph Delappe, Martine Vaugel had sculpted Gandhi in various mode and various sizes. New York figurative sculptor Bob Clyatt has created sculpture of Gandhi (19"H 12"D 13"W) sitting in traditional padmasana in bronze and resin. Joseph Delappe (1963–) who is famous for the intervention pieces that explore contemporary issues through new media installations and interactive gaming performances, built the 17ft life-size sculpture using cardboard, and then recreated the salt march with the help of a treadmill at the Eyebeam gallery in New York City in 2008. Martine Vaugel, the French-American sculptress who founded 'passionist

Gautam Paul, Embassy of India, Washington

D.C.Bronze Bob Clyatt 19" H 12" D 13" W, bronze and resin

movement in art had also portrayed Gandhi in a very compassionate mood. Shane Hodge sculpted a series on historical busts of people who have contributed greatly to humanity.

Ratnabali Kant, Bronze, Nicosia Republic of Cyprus, 2005

Gautam Paul, Bronze, Almaty, Kazakhstan

In this series Gandhi was portrayed in bronze (20"+12"+11"); with a smile in his face he looks dignified and compassionate.

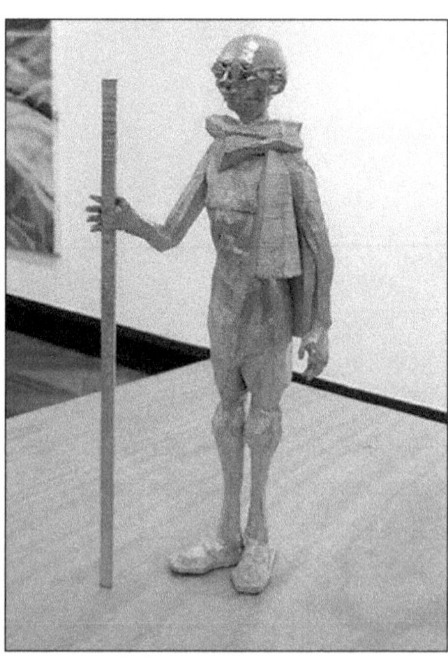

Joseph Delappe, Cardboard Gandhi, New York, 2008–2009

Gold Gandhi, 2008 3D print/gold leaf, 12"

In 2005, a Gandhi bust Sculpted in bronze by Ms. Ratnabali Kant has been installed right next to the Parliament building in Cyprus. Gandhi statue became an icon sought after by every country so a sculpture created by well-known Chinese painter Yuan Xikun (1944–) was also erected in China on the international friendship forest located in the western part of the Beijing's Chaoyang Park. The statue, 1.08 meters in height and 1 meter in width depicts Gandhi reading a book. He looks more like a Chinese than an Indian. Gopal Krishna Gandhi says, "He looks like he could be a friend of one of the three Chinese poets Vikram Seth has translated. Gandhi is reading the book with care and — worry. What is the

Martine Vaugel, 30cm tall × 22xm × 20xm.

Shane Hodges

Resin on Bronze Yuan Xikun, Chaoyang Park, Beijing

book? One will never know but if Yuan's passion for the physical environment is anything to go by, the book is one that was unwritten in Gandhi's time — Martin Rees's deeply troubling work on the future of humankind — Our Final Century"[246].

Soviet sculptor Dmitry Ryabichev (1926–1995) sculpted Gandhi in 1984 as a thinker delving deep inwardly with unusual hand gesture that creates pensive albeit inspiring ambiance all around. It may remind us Rodin's The Thinker. His sculptor son Alexander Ryabichev has made a replica of his father's creation and on the eve of the celebration of the first International Non-Violence Day on 2nd October, 2007, presented it to the Indian Embassy in Moscow as a token of his respect for the country and its people.

---

246 https://epaper.telegraphindia.com/calcutta/2018-10-21/71/Page-12.html (accessed on 18.09.2022)

Dmitry Ryabichev, Bronze, Gandhi Darshan Complex, Delhi

Replica, bronze, 15.3 × 22.9 inches

Alexander Ryabichev, 2007 Gorky Park, Moscow, 1984

In 2003, Tinka Christopher's bronze sculpture of Gandhi was unveiled in Gandhi square in the city centre of Johannesburg on the eve of Mahatma's birth day on 2nd October. This 2.5 meter statue depicts Gandhi as a young lawyer in his gown, over a suit and tie, with a book under his arm, looking commemorating the four terms of imprisonment imposed on Gandhi in determined

Tinka Christopher, Bronze, Johannesburg. 2003

Gautam Paul, Bronze, Fort Prison Complex, 2012

but bit contemplative. This statue is erected upon a 5m Tall plinth, making it an imposing presence in the space. This 2.5 meter bronze figure was commissioned by the City of Johannesburg, unveiled in 2003. There is another Gandhi bust, sculpted by Gautam Paul at the Fort Prison complex at today's Constitution Hill together with a permanent exhibition South Arica that was unveiled in 2012.

Nándor Wagner (1922–1997), a Hungarian sculptor created Garden of Philosophy, a group of eight statues for better mutual understanding in the world in which one of them is Gandhi Ji. Three complete sets were cast one for Japan, one for Hungary and one for USA. The sculpture, created in 1997, the year sculptor

Nándor Wagner, Garden of Philosophy

Gellért Hill, Budapest, 2001

died but found its lonely hillside home in Hungary on the Gellért Hill and was unveiled on 18th of October, 2001. The artist's aim in this work was to promote mutual understanding among the world's religions and faith. In this majestic work, there are eight statues composing one orbit of five founders of religion—

Abraham, Jesus, Buddha, Laozi, and Akhenaten and three icons—Mahatma Gandhi, Daruma Daishi (aka Bodhidharma), and Saint Francis— are placed facing them in a row. Gandhi's statue is the most recognizable and contemporary. The overall composition of the sculptures looks somewhat serene and East Asian, maybe it's because artist spent his last 25 years of life in Japan. The impact of this work on lookers is stimulating.

There is one very unique two-sided bust of Mahatma Gandhi in Pietermaritzburg, South Africa in which on one side is the young lawyer, suited with tie as he first arrived in South Africa while the other side is bespectacled with his khadi chaddar as he popularly known. This sculpture denotes the making of Mahatma. The bust is named the Birth of Satyagraha since this was the place where the idea of Satyagraha first struck to his mind. This unique bust was conceptualized and done by Birad Rajaram Yajnik and his twenty professionals associates. As the curator

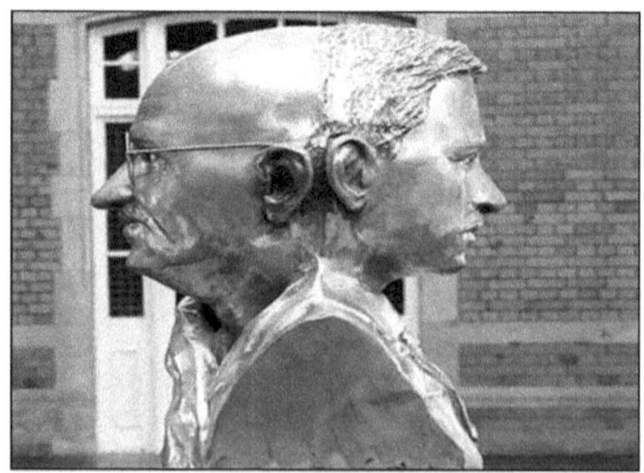

Birad Rajaram Yajnik & others,
Birth of Satyagraha, Two sided bust, Pietermaritzburg, 2018

of Mahatma Gandhi Digital Museums and Managing Director of Visual Quest India, Yajnik explains that this bust is a multimedia installation and Our intention was to create a bust that speaks, is mapped from images of his face and will remain for 100 years, and by the end of it, all these challenges were met, so we find near the statue a Smart Sound Kinetic Power Device Walk up to it and wind it up to hear Gandhi's favourite bhajans Vaishnava Jana To, Raghupati Raghav Raja Ram and a speech in Gandhi's own voice."[247] This is somehow extension or some further exploration in the digital multimedia of those kind of works that was initiated by the artist like Joseph Delappe and others. Recently in August 2022, on the eve of 80th anniversary of Quit India Movement, one statue of Gandhi Ji was made out of recycled waste plastic, that is 20 feet high, 6 feet long, 6 feet wide and it is weighing 1, 150 kg. Executing Mahatma Gandhi's vision of Independent India with cleanliness — in spirit and in truth,

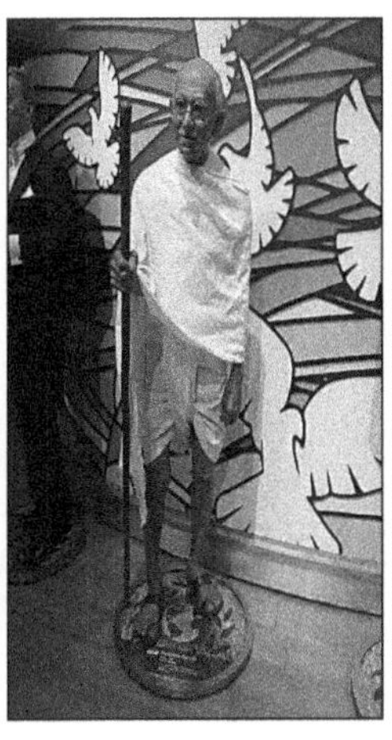

Recycled Plastic, 20 feet high, 6 feet long, 6 feet wide, NOIDA	Wax Statue, Madame Tussaud's Museum, London	Cement Plaster Bust, Dhaka Ghanshyampur, Shahjahanpur, UP

the Noida administration with HCL has created this statue using 1,000 kg plastic waste collected from around the city. Now

---

247 https://www.edexlive.com/happening/2018/sep/27/from-facial-recognition-to-3d-printing-everything-that-went-into-mahatma-gandhis-two-sided-bust-in-4038.html (accessed on 9.11.2022)

iconography of Gandhi turns into such a colossal enterprise that medium is no bar, be it plastic, wax, cement, stone, marble or wood. There are thousand and thousand statues are installed in dusty villages square or community grounds in rural India and as Gandhi ji's grandson Gopal Krishna Gandhi rightly pointed out that, " It will be found in no art catalogue, no list of Gandhi-sculptures. It will not be considered 'art'. In its frank depiction of the un-handsome looks of its subject it can have no peer. It shows him just as he was, only more un-prepossessing. It has been sculpted by what may be called the sculpting genius of our people. I refer to the 'very ordinary' cement-plaster bust of Gandhi that stands on dusty pedestals in the cities, towns and villages of India. This bust, for all its rusticity, says something vastly simpler but so much rarer than do the great bronzes and rock-cuts. It says, simply, 'This man told no lies, was honest, bore no hatred towards anyone'."[248]

This is simply true.

Studying Gandhi or Gandhism as *Subject-matter* in any art form should neither be a purely diachronic nor purely synchronic enterprise since not only *subject* is not time- bound and historical but *matter* too changes according to our point of view or point of reference. No wonder, like true classic as our short survey suggests, Gandhi and art as *subject* and *matter* are both reinventing itself with changing times and this is the reason it is still live and stimulating.

---

248 https://epaper.telegraphindia.com/calcutta/2018-10-21/71/Page-12.html   (accessed   on 18.09.2022)

8

INDIAN CLASSICAL MUSIC: ADAPTING OR DETERIORATING

Generally, it is said that Indian Classical music is intrinsically transcendental, so it has no temporal dimension and is hardly gets affected by the changing sensibilities of its listening public. But is it so? Let us conjure up what happens these days in any music concert: Like a film star the celebrity artiste arrives and his arrival is decorously heralded. Against a background of big banners of sponsors and their campaigns the stage is beautifully decorated in an ethnic set-up vibrating with colourful flowers and smiling sari-clad women and fragrance wafting all around.

The artist is now garlanded by female hands and now there is another round of thunderous applause. The artiste starts something in vilambit ektaal and soon after a few moments, the tempo rises and a duel with the tabla- player ensues until there is an infuriating finale followed by an outburst of applause. Then the artist cools down and after some gimmicks he/she concludes with a small piece of Bhajan, Thumri or dhun and so ends the recital.

This scene[249] is indicative of so many things—first of all, it reveals the emergence of an altogether different relationship between the performers, the patrons and the listening public. At the time of the princely states and darbar the patrons were kings and local rulers and the audience consisted mainly of the small elite whose capability to appreciate the nuances of the classical music was superb. They were highly conversant with the idioms of and esoteric styles of distinct classical music. so for them, it was but natural to encourage the various gharana's distinct ways of mixing alapa, layakari, tana and composition. In such an environment various styles in kheyal and dhrupad had flourished where an artist could be highly benefited and appreciated as a master of the distinct idiom of his gharana. But with the demise of the princely states and their courts everything changed —not only did the long standing infrastructure of the classical music (gharanadari, guru-shishya parampara, court patronage) vanish, but the knowledgeable listeners also started disappearing.

In this changed scenario, musicians had to look for a new patronage. They found it after independence in the beginning from All India Radio, and later Doordarshan and also from the corporate sectors. Today the biggest promoters of music are corporate giants and obviously their interests lie not in promoting music and artists but in improving their public relations, increasing the popularity of their product and attracting the benign eyes of the government. Now the

---

249 This is typical Hindustani Kheyal scene but in essence the Carnatic scene is no different

promotion and propagation of music has become a commercial proposition, like mainstream cinema, where *taste* of the audience is the only criterion. In this scheme of commerce, they have started glamourizing musicians like film stars, creating thereby a star-system of a chosen dozen from whose services they are operating their games of commerce. Our idiot box is also helping them under the banner of the New Economic Policy. For example in the T. V. serials on musicians heavy stress is given on their lavish life-styles and mannerism, and less on their musical styles and nuances. Now we have concerts/conferences/recitals all the year round in big cities, where star performers are paid highly and the audience can listen music without any entry fee. This is the context in which the above mentioned scene could be located and analyzed.

The new patronage system and public's easy access to music have changed the complexion of the Indian classical music thoroughly. Easy accessibility has really snatched the music's former esotericism and in the words of Walter Benjamin, its aura too[250]. Now the listening public is a motley crowd, most of whom have little or no training of the classical music and its nuances, so the musicians find that their music is being applauded for the kind of renditions never appreciated before by their elders and gurus. This realization has forced them to change their complex styles and conform to the test of the audience in order to acquire wider recognition and salability.

The general listening public has a craze for speed and that has done much harm to the variety and quality of the music. The

---

250 The work of Art in the Age of Mechanical Reproduction in Illuminations, Fontana press, 1992, p215

desire for speed frequently results in a loss of fine intonation. Speed also cannot be achieved in a crooked (vakra) tana; it suits only doubled and quadrupled tones. Consequently this very tana became dominant and other variety of tanas gone astray. Rhythmic variety has also suffered a lot because listening public have no ear for the traditional rhythmic variations; consequently a situation arises where one hardly comes across any variations in *gayaki*, be it Dhrupad or Kheyal. In the name of public demand importance of composition is being neglected and heavy stress on *mukhra* is highlighted as the centre of improvisation. This is true that when entertainment becomes prime concern all that was forbidden for the gayaki -performance in earlier times started getting prominence. To entertain emerging new listening public it has developed its repertoire in which V.H. Deshpande includes: joint performance by two artists; the trial of skills between a singer and an instrument-player; the table-percussionist's mastery of the fastest table-laya (tempo);a singer's excessive tana display totally uncalled for and incomprehensible to the listener's intelligence ;and yet all such antics similar to those of a circus-joker's that win applause but are flippant and excessive from the point of genuine classical music; antics that masquerade as the science of music but are really specimens of fake music."[251] For the old generation now it is quite disheartening to see that there is no diversity of style in presenting the music. Not only has the basic pattern of performance been reduced to a single variety but also the characteristic difference between *gharanas* (music-family) has become very indistinct. Today no artist can claim that his/her presentation is a distinct style of a certain

251 Vamanrao H. Deshpande, Indian Musical Traditions, Popular Prakashan Private Limited, Bombay, second edition 1987, p.121

gharana. What he/she does can be called the amalgamation of the different distinct styles of the former *gharanas*. These days one can observe a clear tilt in the audience's liking towards romantic styles. Ornamentations of thumri has, thus, become common in almost every performance. Not only has *thumri* gayaki witnessed a perceptible decorous change in its style, but also a substantial impact of it is being felt in the rendering of kheyal, Dhrupad too.

The entry of microphone in musical performances has also made a dent on the quality and nature of renderings. Unlike small chamber concerts, big auditorium and pandal need microphone for clear audibility. In the present high-tech era, a musician merely whispers and the technology does the rest. Therefore, there is a shift in voice culture: from strong to soft ones.

Something can be said about the ragas in modern times—some disappear, some emerge and some are created. This is not a new phenomenon. It has always happened and will be happening always in future as per general mood of the age. Thus, if today no one knows raga Deepak, Saratha, Gandhari, Jaldhara etc., is it simply because our age does not need (read understand) it or if some new ragas, that is nothing more than amalgams of old ragas are constantly being created, is it only because of its conformity to the *taste* of our age?. The answer leads to the another question: Indian classical music is adopting or deteriorating?

9

OTHER IN SELF:
AN INDIAN DOCTOR IN CHINA
& A CHINESE HAWKER IN INDIA*

If the construct of other is pre requisite for the construct of self, than how to perceive other in self that consequently leads to the realization of true humanism? The self/other binary seems to be an accepted category of how the modern individual comprehends who is/he is, by recognizing what s/he is not, but what happens when one relates to the other, seeing one's self in others, *or* one behaves differently than one would typically act, causing the self to appear as other in self. The true story of Dr. Dwarkanath Kotnis (1910–1942) and Wang Lu of *Chinni Pheriwala (The Chinese Hawker)* is worth delving in this regard. The life of Dwarkanath Kotnis and the story of Indian congress medical mission to China was chronicled in a book written by K.A. Abbas (1914–1987) titled *And one didn't come back* (1944).

* This is version of a keynote speech in A Literary Dialogue Between China and India at Zhejiang Yuexiu University of Foreign Languages, Shaoxing, China on 25th Oct'2019

Similarly *Chinni Ferriwala* (1943) is a memoir written on a Chinese hawker in Allahabad by Mahadevi Verma (1907–87), renowned Hindi poetess, Feminist and educationist of Gandhian era. What is interesting about both examples is that besides being true stories it was made into films. In the backdrop of Chinese-Japanese war and Indian war of independence, it emphasizes the fact that until we see other in us we will not be able to live a harmonious and fruitful life, in other words —a life is hardly meaningful if it is not lived with the realization of others in us. The chronicler of the life of Dr. Dwarkanath Kotnis, K.A. Abbas rightly mentions in his book: "In the sordid and gruesome record of modern warfare, the only redeeming feature is the humanitarian work of those 'warriors without weapons' who risk all the hazards of the battlefields not to kill but to save, not to inflict wounds but to heal them. This legion of mercy— doctors and nurses and stretcher-bearers is perhaps the only evidence of man's evolution into something better than fratricidal ape."[252]

In Srimad Bhagvat Geeta, Lord Krishna says to Arjuna, अद्वेष्टा सर्वभूतानां मैत्रः करुण एव च । निर्ममो निरहङ्कारः समदुःखसुखः क्षमी [253] (Adveshtâ sarvabhuthânâm Maitrah karuna eva cha/Nirmamô nirahamkârah samadukha sukha ksha mee.) means that He who hates no creature, who is friendly and compassionate to all, who is free from attachment and egoism, balanced in pleasure and pain and forgiving is dear to me. To achieve such a state of being, it again emphasizes that it is necessary to perceive one's self by including other in self.

---

252 K.A.Abbas, And One Did Not Come Back, Sound magazine, 1944, p.13
253 Bhagavad Gita, Chapter 12, Verse 13

Dr. Dwarkanath Kotnis (1910–42) born in a middle class Maharashtrian family from Sholapur on 10th October 1910, he had graduated from the Seth G. S. Medical College, Bombay. In 1938, after the Japanese invasion of China, the communist General Zhu De requested Jawaharlal Nehru to send some medical professionals to China. A medical team of five doctors: Dr. M. Atal from Allahabad, the leader of the mission, M. Cholkar from Nagpur, B.K. Basu and Debesh Mukherjee from Calcutta and Dwarkanath Kotnis was sent to China as the Indian Medical Mission Team in September 1938. The team first arrived in China at the port of Hankou, Wuhan. They were then sent to Yan'an, the revolutionary base at the time in 1939, where they were warmly welcomed by Mao Zedong, Zhu De and other top leaders of the Communist Party, as they were the first medical team to come from another Asian country. Doctor Kotnis stayed in China for almost 5 years working in moving clinics to treat injured soldiers. In 1939, Dr. Kotnis joined the Eighth Route Army, led by Mao Zedong at the Jin-Cha-Ji border near the Wutai Mountain Area. His job as a doctor in firing zone was stressful, especially when there was always an acute short supply of medicines. In one prolonged fight against Japanese troops in 1940, Dr. Kotnis performed operations for up to 72 hours continuously without any rest or sleep. He treated more than 800 injured soldiers during the battle. He was eventually appointed as the Director of the Dr. Bethune International Peace Hospital named after the famous Canadian surgeon Norman Bethune. In 1940, Dr. Kotnis met Guo Qinglan, a nurse at the Bethune Hospital. They first met at the inauguration of Dr. Norman Bethune's tomb and Guo was instantly attracted to the Indian doctor. They got married in December 1941. They had a son on 23 August

1942, who was named Yinhua – meaning India (Yin) and China (Hua), at the suggestion of Nie Rongzhen, a prominent Chinese Communist military leader. The hardship of the stressful job as a battle-line doctor eventually started to take its toll on him and severely damaged his health. Only three months after the birth of his son, epilepsy struck Dr. Kotnis. He died on 9th December 1942, leaving behind his widow Guo Qinglan, and the baby son. Dr. Kotnis was buried in the Heroes Courtyard in Nanquan Village. At that time, Mao Zedong (1893–1976) mourned his death by observing that "The army has lost a helping hand, the nation has lost a friend. Let us always bear in mind his internationalist spirit."[254] Buried in the Heroes Courtyard in Nanquan Village, the life of Dr. Kotnis proves what K.A. Abbas quotes John Donne in the beginning of the chapter Warriors without Weapons in his book *And One Did Not Come Back*: "No man is an island entire of itself; every man is a piece of the continent, a part of the main; any man's death diminishes me, because I am involved in mankind. And therefore never send to know for whom the bell tolls; it tolls for thee."[255] The poem basically talks about how the entire human race is one entity and how we all are responsible for each other. Ernest Hemingway quoted it as the title of his famous novel on the Spanish Civil War. It means simply that we are all humans and what harm comes to one person affects all others. To reflect upon the life and deeds of Dr. Kotnis, Guo Qinglan's memoir *My life with Kotnis* is very important. She graphically recollected everything related to Dr. Kotnis in China; her first encounter with him, her medical apprenticeship, her

---

254 http://www.china.org.cn/china/CPC_95_anniversary/2016-06/27/content   _38756454   .
      htm(accessed on 11.03.2019)
255 K.A. Abbas, ibid, pp122–123

marriage with him and the birth of their only child and later the sad demise of Dr. Kotnis and her son. She has given not only the detailed description of their personal life but accurate life situation of those turbulent times of war where the hardships of battle-front and the ecstasy of serving humanity were going hand in hand with "sincere wishes for eternal friendship between China and India."

In K.A. Abbas words, Guo was "A smart, attractive jolly girl, about five feet tall and with a round moon-like face, wearing thick glasses, she was a teacher of nursing at the Bethune Medical School of which Kotnis was the Principal. Working as she was under Kotnis, it is not difficult to imagine how she felt drawn towards this brave young man from India who had sacrificed so much to serve her country. Admiration ripened into love, and to Kotnis it was one more link binding him to the soil of China. Kuo Ching Lan, unlike most Chinese girls, was not shy. She could speak English fluently and together they had many talks and discussions about India, about China, about the world, about themselves!"[256] She herself recollected all these details of their relationship later: "On 21 June 1940, the inauguration ceremony of the mausoleum of the great internationalist soldier, Dr. Bethune was solemnly held at the south of Junchneg in Tang County, Hebei province. During the welcome reception, the staff of our Health School was sitting right in front and we could see clearly Kotnis on the stage. He was of moderate height and had those sparkling bright big eyes on his brownish face that made an unforgettable impression on others. Don't know why, Kotnis' not so proficient speech in Chinese deeply attracted

---

256 K.A.Abbas, ibid, pp.122–123

my schoolmates and me. His sincere sympathy for the Chinese people and his anti-war resolve was so infectious that one and all were infected by it. I was completely mesmerized by his speech. Probably I was listening with such rapt attention that he noticed me. Unexpectedly he smiled at me, my heart echoed it with gentle flutters. I shyly bowed my head lest he discover a youthful girl's secret. On my way back home, Kotnis' image, elegance, zeal and especially those big eyes, thoroughly got engraved in my mind. I contemplated while walking: Why should an Indian youth leave the comfortable living in India and travel all the way to China to bear hardships. He attracted me like a magnet, we often sang, exercised and worked together. Since my English was good, we often used English to chat. We liked each other and became very good friends."[257] She remembered her son Yinhua with these words: "He was a handsome boy. He had his father's large eyes and my fair skin."…"Time seems to drag on, flowers blossom and wither. Time is like running water, slowly and swiftly it passes by, if I think of it, ninety years have already passed. Over 32000 days and nights of these ninety years is just a twinkling in this vast universe, however, for an old lady like me who has survived the hardships and frustrations of life, the journey of life has indeed been very long and endless. The episodes of my recollections are like winter snowflakes dancing and fluttering in front of my eyes and the scenes of the yesteryears appear as if they are the acts of yesterday…"[258]

The biopic made in 1946 on Dr. Kotnis by V. Shantaram as *The Eternal Tale of Doctor Kotnis* in English and *Doctor Kotnis Ki*

---

257 My Life With Kotnis, Manak Publications PVT. Ltd. Delhi, First Edition, 2006, pp.56–58
258 Ibid, p 1

Amar Kahani in Hindi portrays the protagonist of the film as a person who defines his role in this world as someone who serves his nation by serving suffering humanism wherever it exists— in this case, it was China. Consequently Dr. Kotnis realizes other in self while serving injured armies under the ongoing Japanese onslaught. Reportedly he proclaims in one place, "Of course, I may die or become disabled. However, if I have to die for liberating the people from the iron claws of the fascists, the Indian people would be happy. You (to Guo Qinglan) me, and our yet to be born child would all be happy, for I would have laid down my life for the glorious cause of humanity."[259]

This was truly a life dedicated for harmony and peace in the world and the film was unambiguous and direct in its approach. V. Shantaram as director and as protagonist of this film was considered quite successful in putting forward convincingly the anti-war sentiments and ideas of humanism of his fellow countryman. Here internationalism was portrayed as natural corollary of nationalism and private domain was extended right up to the boundary of public sphere. The film is successful in creating the emotional environment where idealism does not appear dry and dusty but as a way of life, that may give meaning to our life. It was ironic that the film of V. Shantaram was re-edited in 1950s and made into a typical American exploitation film as *Nightmare in Red China*, where china is shown overrun not by Japanese but by communists and where Chinese nationalist guerillas were fighting the red.[260] This is also revealing to know what *Rotten Tomatoes*, an American review-

---

259 Ibid, p 354

260 see, Immortal tale or nightmare? Dr Kotnis between art and exploitation, Neepa Majumdar
    Journal of South Asian Popular Culture, Volume 6, 2008 - Issue 2, Pages 141–159

aggregation website for film and television, describes about this film: "Made at the height of the Cold War, this Indian film dramatizes the perils of communism and what's in store for the West if communism ever prevails. An Indian doctor travels to China to aid a band of anti-communist guerrillas. While there, he witnesses such atrocities as communist doctors performing germ war experiments on civilians, and communist soldiers raping nuns and bayoneting priests."[261] It is a glaring example of misappropriation where a noble mission was turned into a vehicle for winning a heinous ideological war (cold). This act was antithetical to whatever Dr. Kotnis and his team stood for —it was perceiving and propagating as if other is hell, not in a Sartrean sense of existentialism but quite literally.

Let's take another example of Chinese hawker Wang Lu of *Chinni Ferriwala* who like Dr. Kotnis, is not a high profile state guest of a country but a simple hawker struggling for his survival in a foreign land. He instinctively perceives himself out here not as a foreigner and rebuts whoever thinks he is a foreigner. He simply emphasizes flatness of his nose, colour of his skin as a marker to differentiate him from the Englishman and says, "I am not a foreigner...No English...I am a Chinaman"[262]. He reminds us the sentiments expressed by Dr. Kotnis who has reportedly proclaimed in China that, "I cannot be treated as a foreigner!"[263]

Humans are inherently social animals and trying for relationships with other individuals is not unusual. Various conceptualizations of human relationships have been proposed.

---

261 https://www.rottentomatoes.com/m/nightmare_in_red_china

262 See, Mrinal sen's Neel Aakasher Neeche

263 quoted in My Life with Kotnis, ibid, p.354

Social psychologists introduced a cognitive view point by postulating that the other is to some extent included in the self, creating overlapping cognitive structures with the other and self-disclosure is argued to be one of the main predictors of inclusion of the other in the self[264]. In Mahadevi Verma's memoir the Chinese hawker discloses every vital details of his life to her —death of his mother, father's second marriage and his demise, cruelty of his step-mother, culminating in forcing his elder sister to prostitution and then sudden disappearance of his sister, his long struggle for survival in underworld and finally his two cherished wishes in life, first to become a honest person and second to find out his long lost sister. This is a life like parable and Mahadevi Verma comments that fulfilling first wish rests entirely on him but for the second wish he prays Gautama Buddha every day. Mrinal Sen's film *Neel Akasher Niche* deviates from Mahadevi Verma's account and not only the locale of the story was changed from Allahabad to Calcutta but self-disclosure by the protagonist of the memoir turned into flashback memories of the lone hero in the film- narrative and in this process the human bond between narrator and listener could not be evolved as strongly and as organically as it was developed in the memoir. The aim of the film, it seems was different as Mrinal Sen's official website introduces this film in such words: Set in turbulent 'thirties, it is the story of a poor Chinese hawker selling his merchandise, China silk, in the streets of Calcutta. That was the time when China was repulsing the brutal attack of the militarist Japan. That was the time when an outraged Rabindranath Tagore wrote to his friend in Japan,

---

264 Aron, A., Aron, E. N., & Smollan, D. (1992). Inclusion of other in the self-scale and the structure of interpersonal closeness. Journal of Personality and Social Psychology, 63(4), 596–612.

the great poet Noguchi: "I wish your countrymen, whom I love so much, not success but remorse."[265] Unlike memoir the film has strong political overtones and that is the reason why we find the change in emphasis. Finally it can be stated that while Dr. Kotnis and Wang Lu perceived themselves not as foreigners in a foreign land by emphasizing inherent similarities among humans and their ability to include others in self; their counterparts, chiefly Guo Qinglan and Mahadevi Verma as a foster sister and as wife developed a tender and responding relationship with them on the ground of pure human emotions and compassion. Mahadevi Verma concludes her memoir in these words: "I don't know the one, who was so impoverish, orphan, long separated from his only sister, my Chinese brother, whether he has reached China or not —his sole destination of all his hope and affection, I don't have any proof for that but my good sense says so."[266]

The story of Guo Qinglan and Mahadevi Verma postulates the very process of *other in self* to achieve true Humanism.

---

265 http://mrinalsen.org/neel_akasherr_niche.html(accessed on 10.10.2021)
266 Lines of Memory (1943)

10

SELF IN PERFORMANCE: RITUPARNO GHOSH AS CHITRANGADA*

Sometimes self is discovered through performances and since self is not centered around a single identity and it is heterogeneous, fluid and liminal in nature, performances ought to be multi-layered, symptomatic and self-revealing. Performance, as we all know is all about presenting oneself before the world with a consciousness of it. Indian film director Rituparno Ghosh, an icon of LGBT community in India performed several roles like writing screenplays, advertisements and songs, acting in films (like *Arekti Premer Galpo, Memories in March & Chitrangada*) editing magazines (*Anandalok, Sambad Pratidin*) anchoring TV chat shows (*Ebong Rituparno & Ghosh and Company)* commenting on literary, gender and cultural issues, designing sets, jewellery and fashion shows, walking the ramp,

---

*   This is a version of a paper presented in the 24th European Conference on South Asian Studies at University of Warsaw, Poland on 29th July 2016.

elocution, besides directing films and TV serials. He was really a multifarious performer who has discovered his self through varied performances in a much sustained and evolved manner, as film maker Aparna Sen said, "It is as if he were creating himself from scratch in his own laboratory—right from the point of choosing his name to becoming a formidable film-maker who flaunted his trans-sexuality with fearless aplomb."[267]

Rituparno Ghosh (1963–2013), was born in a Bengali Hindu family on 31 August 1963 in Kolkata. His father, Sunil Ghosh, was a documentary film maker and painter and his mother was also an artist. He completed his schooling at South Point High School, and earned a degree in economics from Jadavpur University, Kolkata. He started his career as copywriter in Ram Ray's advertising agency 'Response' in Kolkata. He made his first documentary film' Vande Matram' in 1990 and first feature film 'Hirer Angti' in 1992 and then on in twenty years time of his life he made twenty feature films[268] in which Chitrangada is the most expressive and symptomatic of his self.

Film Chitrangada (2012) starts before casting with a caption:

"Mahabharata describes Chitrangada as a beautiful princess whom Arjuna was married with.

---

267 Sangeeta Datta, Kaustav Bakshi, Rohit K. Dasgupta, (eds.), Rituparno Ghosh: Cinema, Gender and Art, Routledge, New Delhi, London, New York, First Published 2016, p264

268 Hirer Angti (The Diamond Ring), 1992; Unishe April (19 April), 1994; Dahan (Crossfire), 1997; Bariwali (The Lady of the House), 1999; Asukh (Malaise), 1999; Utsab (The Festival), 2000; Titli (The First Monsoon Day), 2002; Shubho Mahurat 2003; Chokher Bali (A Passion play), 2003; Raincoat, 2004; Antarmahal, Views of the Inner Chamber), 2005; Dosar (The Companion), 2006; The Last Lear, 2007; Khela (Get Set Go), 2008; Shob Charitro Kalponik (Afterwards), 2009; Abahoman (The Eternal), 2010; Arekti Premer Galpo, 2010; Nouka Dubi/Kashmakash (The Boat Wreck), 2011; Memories in March 2011; Chitrangada (The Crowning Wish, 2012; Satyanveshi (The Truth Seeker), 2013.

"Tagore's Chitrangada is an Amazon worrier in a quest to discover her gender identity.

"From the work of Tagore comes a very personal interpretation..."

Chitrangada is a character of the epic Mahabharata that was reformulated by Rabindranath Tagore (1861–1941) in a dance-drama *Chitra* (1913). In Mahabharata Chitrangada is a Manipuri princess who falls in love with Arjun and subsequently gets married and bears a son from him but Tagore made her an Amazon worrier who is in a quest to discover her gender identity. The first scene of Tagore's dance drama opens with the dialogue between Madana, and Chitrangada, where after meeting Arjuna she persuades the God of Eros to make her a feminine beauty so Arjuna falls for her:

Chitra: I am Chitra, the daughter of the kingly house of Manipur. With godlike grace Lord Shiva promised to my royal grandsire an unbroken line of male descent. Nevertheless, the divine word proved powerless to change the spark of life in my mother's womb—so invincible was my nature, woman though I be.

Madana: I know, that is why thy father brings thee up as his son. He has taught thee the use of the bow and all the duties of a king.

Chitra: Yes, that is why I am dressed in man's attire and have left the seclusion of a woman's chamber. I know no feminine wiles for winning hearts. My hands are strong to bend the bow, but I have never learnt cupid's archery, the plays of eyes.... For a single day make me superbly beautiful, even as beautiful as was the sudden blooming of love in my heart. Give me but one brief day of perfect beauty, and I will answer for the days that follow.[269]

---

269 Collected Poems and Plays of Rabindranath Tagore, Rupa Publications India Pvt.Ltd.New Delhi, Fifth Impression, 2011, pp.153–156

But after getting Arjuna's love soon she realizes the futility and falsehood of the borrowed beauty and subsequent identity, she says to Arjuna:

Arjuna, tell me true, if now at once, by some magic I could shake myself free from this voluptuous softness, this timid bloom of beauty shrinking from the rude and healthy touch of the world, and fling it from my body like borrowed clothes, would you be able to bear it? If I stand up straight and strong with the strength of a daring heart spurning the wiles and arts of twining weakness, if I hold my head high like a tall young mountain fir, no longer trailing in the dust like a liana, shall I then appeal to man's eye?[270]

This was the Tagore's Chitrangada's conflict and tension between her sexuality and gender role that attracted Rituparno Ghosh to reinterpret it in his film in the context of his own 'lived experiences' and his queer positioning.[271]

Rituparno's film starts with a conversation between protagonists Rudra Chatterjee, a gay choreographer lying on a hospital bed for his sex reassignment surgery and his counselor Shubho who, as we know at the end of the narrative does not exist in the 'reality' but can be taken as a voice of his unconscious.

---

270 Ibid, p170

271 Chitrangada was among the films screened at the Kashish Mumbai International Queer Festival, held in Mumbai from 22–26 May 2012. Festival director Sridhar Rangayan said Arekti Premer Golpo, Memories in March and Chitrangada "question issues of identity and sexuality in a very Indian way, and talk about contemporary issues within a mainstream framework". http://www.livemint.com/Consumer/NGQP6dAn14VkftVnA3FBbL/Filmmaker-Rituparno-Ghosh-49-dies-of-cardiac-arrest.html (accessed on 23.07.2016)

It seems conversation is intended to continue, in Freudian sense what is "phenomenologically discontinuous"[272]

Conversation begins only when counselor assures him that he is free to talk with him whenever and whatever he feels like talking, be his poems or writings, he agrees after initial reluctance to hire a counselor for this major surgery. The first piece the protagonist narrates to him is:

"It had to be in heir what all the father knew to carry on the name and family pride so the training began. The child to be a girl or a boy—they did not even ask or want to know… children have dreams beyond their parent's expectations and they wish on stars and fallen eyelashes. Sometimes wishes come true and unexpectedly come to life and turn the everyday inside out."

Counselor: "Is that an introduction, a prelude, before the show begins?"

Rudra: "yes I guess so"

Counselor: "Will they link it to 'Chitrangada' the Tagore opera?

Rudra: Do I need to tell the story from the start? They will get it, won't they?

Counselor: Isn't it too autobiographical? Or is that what you want?

---

272 The argument is based on the observation that the stream of consciousness is phenomenologically discontinuous. It is riddled with "gaps", such as the dramatic daily occurrence of sleep. During sleep, our normal conscious mental life ceases, and yet is restored with no loss of coherence or identity when we awaken. Another example, singled out by Freud, is the experience of giving up work on a seemingly intractable intellectual problem and putting the problem out of mind only to have the answer later occur to one "out of the blue". The Freud Encyclopedia: Theory, Therapy And Culture, Edward Erwin, Rutledge, New York, London, 2002, p.579.

Rudra: you say that because you know me. Ok, if I ever write an autobiography I will dedicate it to you— "To Shubho, my counsellor". All right.

Two things are worth noting here—first Chitrangada is autobiographical and second if wishes regarding one's sexuality and gender role go against training/socialization, subsequently 'everyday turns inside out.'

Rudra discusses Tagore's 'Chitrangada' with Shubho to understand the character for her true characterization in his upcoming production but it seems consequently, more so for understanding himself more closely and more intimately. In one place he confesses to Shubho about his production of Chitrangada:

"it has gloss, spectacle but whether it had the soul of Chitrangada I am not sure and I still don't know her well enough…a princess raised as a son by her father wants to become feminine so she does but does her father accepts her new identity?"

In one of the scene, Rudra, while rehearsing for the staging of Chitrangada in the film, interprets amongst cast and crew of the production that, *"Chitrangada is the story of wish (ichcher Galpo) …her father's wishes verses her own …Chitrangada is a story of desire …that you can choose your gender"*

In life, Rituparno Ghosh emphasized time and again that, *"we often have to play out gender-roles that we may not want to."*[273] Here comes the 'performativity' of gender trouble. In the film choreographer Rudra Chatterjee realizes the essential nature of

---

273 Sangeeta Datta, Kaustav Bakshi, Rohit K. Dasgupta, (eds.), Rituparno Ghosh: Cinema, Gender and Art, Routledge, New Delhi, London, New York, First Published 2016, p238

the performativity of gender: anticipation of a home conjures the concept of a family with a husband, a wife and a child. Judith Butler writes: *"I originally took my clue on how to read the performativity of gender from Jacques Derrida's reading of Kafka's 'Before the Law'. There the one who waits for the law, sits before the door of the law, attributes a certain force to the law for which one waits. The anticipation of an authoritative disclosure of meaning is the means by which that authority is attributed and installed: the anticipation conjures its object.*[274]

Generally it is believed that sexuality and gender are two distinct categories while former represents the body's anatomy and physiological workings the later signifies social forces that mold behavior but it is also been argued that, "What bodily signals and functions we define as male or female come already entangled in our ideas about gender."[275]

---

274 Judith Butler, Gender Trouble: Feminism and the subversion of Identity, Preface (1999) Routledge, New York, London, Reprint 2010

275 Our bodies are too complex to provide clear-cut answers about sexual difference. The more we look for a simple physical basis for "sex," the more it becomes clear that "sex" is not a pure physical category. What bodily signals and functions we define as male or female come already entangled in our ideas about gender. Consider the problem facing the International Olympic Committee. Committee members want to decide definitively who is male and who is female. But how? Could the IOC use muscle strength as some measure of sex? In some cases. But the strengths of men and women, especially highly trained athletes, overlap. (Remember that three women beat Hermann Ratjen's high jump). And although Maria Patin͂o fit a commonsense definition of femininity in terms of looks and strength, she also had testes and a Y chromosome. But why should these be the deciding factors?

The IOC may use chromosome or DNA tests or inspection of the breasts and genitals to ascertain the sex of a competitor, but doctors faced with uncertainty about a child's sex use different criteria. They focus primarily on reproductive abilities (in the case of a potential girl) or penis size (in the case of a prospective boy). If a child is born with two X chromosomes, oviducts, ovaries, and a uterus on the inside, but a penis and scrotum o the outside, for instance, is the child a boy or a girl? Most doctors declare the child a girl, despite the penis, because of her potential to give birth, and intervene using surgery and

Rudra decided to go for sex reassignments surgery as his lover Partho (another name of Arjuna) loves children and same sex parents can't adopt child in India but the question remains unanswered how his sexual identity is going to change his gender especially when he himself reiterated it in front of his lover that:

"Fortunately my art form is not gender bound. My dance is not limited by my gender and neither is my identity."

He considered his art and identity gender free or androgynous. One of the major reasons for his attraction towards Rabindranath Tagore was 'androgynous quality' of his writing. In one of his interviews he emphasized that,

"There's always been a lot of speculation about me on approaching femininity... whether I am going in for a sex change or a breast augmentation. All kinds of speculation. But I was never embarrassed. If I want to change my identity by changing my sex, I would be the first person to let the world know about my new identity. I consider myself privileged because of my gender fluidity, the fact that I am in between.

"I don't consider myself a woman and I don't want to become a woman. I can wear kurta pyjama and direct a film; I can also wear kajal and jewellery and attend a social do.... The concept of unisex has been monopolized by women. Women can wear men's clothes. The problem arises when men wear women's clothes. Whatever I wear has always been worn by men. Wearing things like earrings

---

hormones to carry out the decision. Choosing which criteria to use, in determining sex, and choosing to make the determination at all, are social decisions for which scientists can offer no absolute guidelines.

Sexing the Body, Anne Fausto-Sterling, Basic Books, New York, first edition 2000, pp.4–5

and necklaces has always been a part of our sartorial history and tradition. These were tagged as feminine frills during colonial rule and I don't see anything wrong in reinstating it. My point is why shouldn't I celebrate my sexuality?[276]

In a poignant scene in the film his mother talking about his sexuality to his father says: *"Nature dictates what is natural. It has its own desires. If we had been able to accept ...what was natural for him he would not be lying there under the surgeon's knife"*

It is true that all through his life he suffered some kind of ostracism on this count. In one place he confesses to Shubho:

"Actually *I'd suffered ostracism myself for being effeminate, people made fun of me."*

When Bengali comedian Mir made mimicry of him, Rituparno Ghosh rebuked him in one of the episode of *Ghosh and Company* on the *Star Jalsa* channel:

Have you ever thought that whenever you mimic me, so many effeminate men in Kolkata, in Bengal feel ashamed, feel humiliated?"

"I can carry off my jewellery with such flamboyance it doesn't matter to me. But there are many people who feel tremendous shame and stigma about this, who don't have the courage to wear jewellery, or the guts to wear kajal. I can live life on my terms, Mir. But they cannot."[277]

---

276 The Telegraph, Kolkata, Wednesday, December 22, 2010 http://www.telegraphindia.com/1101222/jsp/entertainment/story_13330745.jsp (accessed on 23.07.2016)

277 http://www.firstpost.com/bollywood/an-icon-beyond-labels-man-woman-or-rituparno-830493.html (accessed on 23.07.2016)

This statement can be testified by one of his own queer elder Chapal Bhaduri [278] when he said:

"I have acted in female roles for decades. But it has always been on stage. I would never have dared to go around dressed as a woman in public like Ritu did. I admire him for his courage to defy the world and be himself"[279]

But defying the world and be himself presupposes some kind of defying and recognizing our contradictions and paradoxes also and the three text messages sent by Shubho to him is quite symptomatic of it: first message was, "If driving in a drunken state is not allowed, why do bars have parking lots?"; second one was, "Everybody wants to go to Heaven, but no one wants to die"; and the last was, "Why do call a building a building even after it is complete?". First two quizzes were considered 'interesting and profound' but last one was answered directly in a utterly surreal environment of dawn when night meets morning (unconscious meets conscious) in a deserted seashore where only his lover and dream house were present and, nurses were waiting for doing preparation for his final surgery; answer came as if an oracle: *"No transaction is ever complete, since it is an ongoing process..."*

It is clear from the context that he, like a classic tragic hero knew his 'fate' or destiny but tried to overcome it by the human intervention—in this case by choosing to go for sex reassignment surgery but resulted in a paradox—is it his fate

---

278 Chapal Bhaduri, a transgender actor of Bengali folk theatre 'jatra' known as 'Chapal Rani'for his female impersonation was the subject on which 'Arekti Premer Galpo' film was made — In this film Rituparno as Abhiroop Sen,a gay film maker tries to make a documentary on his life and realizes the similarities and dissimilarities of the subject with his own life.

279 http://timesofindia.indiatimes.com/city/kolkata/Admire-Rituparno-Ghosh-for-courage-to-defy-world-Chapal-Bhaduri/articleshow/20357753.cms (accessed on 23.07.2016)

or free will which could be considered the prime reason for his sufferings, more in his life and perhaps less in this film where he abandons the proposed surgery for vaginal reconstruction after breast implants whereas doing the same in life he paid the price by giving his life itself.[280]

Now the moot question is: Is it a case where performance in life could not proceed from art or is it a testimony of a conclusion that if your aim is 'heaven', essentially you have to 'die'

---

280 Rituparno suffered from diabetes mellitus type 2 for ten years, and pancreatitis for five years. He experienced insomnia and had been taking medication for it. According to Dr Rajiv Seal of Fortis Hospitals, who had been his physician for almost two decades, Rituparno was also facing complications from hormone treatments after abdominoplasty and breast implants operations which he underwent for his role in Kaushik Ganguly's film, 'Arekti Premer Golpo', in which he played a transgender filmmaker with a bisexual lover.

280 Ghosh died at his Kolkata residence on 30 May 2013, following a massive heart attack. His attendants, Dileep and Bishnu, found him lying unconscious in bed. Nilanjana Sengupta, a neighbour, sent for Dr. Nirup Ray, who declared Ghosh dead. Ghosh was 49 years old.

https://en.wikipedia.org/wiki/Rituparno_Ghosh (accessed on 23.07.2016)

BIBLIOGRAPHY

Abdul Halim Sharaar, Lucknow The Last Phase of the Oriental Culture in the Lucknow Omnibus, OUP, New Delhi, India, 2001

Acharya Brihaspati, Musalmaan aur Bhartiya Sangeet, Rajkamal Prakashan, Delhi, 2nd edition, 1982

Acharya Brihaspati, Sangeet Chintamani, bhaag 2, Brihaspati Publication, New Delhi, 1987

Aditya Behl and Wendy Doniger (Tr. And ed.) The Magic Doe: Qutban Suhravardi's Mirigavati, Oxford University Press, USA, 2012

Adya Rangacharya, Natyasastra, English Translation with Critical Notes, Munshiram Manoharlal Publishers Pvt.Ltd. Fourth edition, 2003

Anand Coomaraswamy, Hindi Ragmala Texts, in Journal of the American Oriental Society, vol. 43, 1923

Anand Coomaraswamy, The Mirror of Gesture, Munshiram Manoharlal, Delhi, fourth edition 1987

Anand K. Coomaraswamy, Art & Swadeshi, Munshiram Manoharlal Pvt Ltd. Second edition 1994

Anand Kumaraswami, Rajput Painting, Motilal Banarasidas, New Delhi, second edition, 1976

Anand Kumaraswamy, Introduction to Indian Art, Munshiram Manoharlal, Delhi, Second edition, feb 1969

Ananda Coomaraswamy, Rajput Painting, vol.1, Motilal Banarasidas, New, New Delhi, 1976

Annal Adichuvattil (In the footsteps of the Mahatma). Kalachuvadu Publications Pvt Ltd, Revised and Expanded 2nd Edition, 2016

Anu Bandopadhyaya M. K. Gandhi: Author, Journalist, Printer, Navajivan Press, Ahmadabad, 1964

Aristotle, Poetics,(Tr. Malcom Heath), Penguin Books, 1996.

Aron, A., Aron, E. N., & Smollan, D. (1992). Inclusion of other in the self-scale and the structure of interpersonal closeness. Journal of Personality and Social Psychology, 63 (4)

B.Chaitnaya Deva, The Music of India: A Scientific Study, Munshram Manoharlal Publishers Pvt. Ltd. 1995.

Bailey, Gauvin A., Art on the Jesuit missions in Asia and Latin America, 1542–1773, University of Toronto press, 1999

Bhabani Bhattacharya, Gandhi the writer, National Book Trust, Delhi, 1969

Clare Sheridan, The Great Little Mahatma in S. Radhakrishnan (ed.), Mahatma Gandhi: Essays and Reflections, George Allen & Unwin Ltd., London, Second (enlarged) edition, 1949

Collected Poems and Plays of Rabindranath Tagore, Rupa Publications India Pvt.Ltd. New Delhi, Fifth Impression, 2011

Collected Works of Mahatma Gandhi, Vol.40, 10 March 1929,

Collected Works of Mahatma Gandhi, Vol.88, 27 May 1947.

Contemporary Indian Literature: A Symposium, Sāhitya Akademi, New Delhi 2nd edition 1959

John Correia-Afonso (ed.), Letters from the Mughal court: the first Jesuit mission to Akbar, 1580–1583, Gujarat Sahitya Prakash, Anand, Bombay, 1980

D.P. Mukherjee, Indian Music, Kutub Publishers, Pune, 1945

Dhiren Gandhi, Prayer and other Sketches of Mahatma Gandhi, Nalanda Publication, Mumbai, 1948.

Dilip Kumar Roy, Among the Great, Jaico Publishing House, Bombay, 1950

Dr. R.S. Nagar (ed.), Natyasastra of Bharatmuni, with the commentary Abhinav Bharati, vol.4, 28/11, Parimal Publications, Delhi, 1998

E. Denison Ross and Eileen Power (ed.) Akbar and the Jesuits, Tulsi Publishing House, New Delhi, 1979

Edward Erwin, The Freud Encyclopedia: Theory, Therapy And Culture, Rutledge, New York, London, 2002

Ganpati Chandra Gupta, Sahityik Nibandh, Lokbharti Prakashan, Allahabad, sixth edition, 1977

Gulammohammed Sheikh, Ruminating on Life of the Medieval Saints, by Benodbehari Mukherjee, The National Gallery of Modern Art, Delhi, date and page no. not mentioned.

Hazariprasad Dwivedi, Kabīr, Rajkamal Prakashan, Delhi. 1994

Hardev Bahri, Rajendra Kumar (ed.), Sursagar-Sateek, first part, Lokbharti Prakashan, Allahabad, revised edition 1991

Harihar NIwas Dwivedi, Madhyadeshiya Bhasha, Vidyamandir Prakashan, Gwalior, Pratham sanskaran, 1955

Hazariprasad Dwivedi, Hindi Sahitya ki Bhumika, Rajkamal Prakashan, New Delhi, edition 2010

Jagannath Das Ratnakar,(ed.), Bihari-Ratnakar, Tara book Agency, Varanasi, 1990

James Lawrence, Raj: The Making and Unmaking of British India, Little Brown and company,

Jo Davidson, Between Sittings: An Informal Autobiography of Jo Davidson, The Dial Press, New York, 1951

Judith Butler, Gender Trouble: Feminism and the subversion of Identity, Preface (1999) Routledge, New York, London

K. M. Varma, Natya, Nritta and Nritya, Orient Longmans, Calcutta, First Published, 1957

K.K. Hebbar, Tulsidas, Abhinav publications, Delhi, 1989

K.M. Munshi, Gujarata and its Literature, Longmans Green & Co. Ltd. Calcutta, 1935

Kailash Chandradev Brihaspati, Bharat ka Sangeet siddhant, Uttar Pradesh Hindi Sansthan, Lucknow, Second Edition, 1991

Kapila Vatsyayan, Classical Dance in Literature and the Arts, Sangeet Natak Akademi, Delhi, 2nd Edition, 1977

Kapila Vatsyayan, Indian Classical Dance, Publication Division, Delhi, 2nd Reprint, 1997

Klaus Ebeling, Ragamala Painting, Ravi Kumar, Paris, 1973

Kshemendra, Suvrattilakam, Chaukhamba Sanskrit Series Office, Varanasi, First Edition, 1968

Lalmani Mishra, Sangeet aur Samaj, Madhukali Prakashan, Bhopal, first edition 2000

Longinus, On the sublime,(Tr.William Rhys Roberts), Garland, 1987.

Luis Fischer, The Life Of Mahatma Gandhi, Indus (Harper Collins), New Delhi, Second Impression1993

M.K. Naik, A History of Indian English Literature, Sāhitya Akademi, New Delhi, 1982

Mac lagan, Edward Douglas, The Jesuits and the Great Mogul, Burns, Oates & Washbourne, London, 1932

Madan Gopal, Tulasi Das, The Bookabode, New Delhi, 1977

Madhu Trivedi, The Emergence of the Hindustani Tradition, Three Essays Collective, Gurgaon, First Edition 2012

Madhu Trivedi, The Emergence of the Hindustani Tradition, Three Essays Collective, Gurgaon, First Edition 2012

Maheep Singh, Adigranth, Rajpal and Sons, Delhi, First Edition, 2009

Mandakranta Bose, Movement and Mimesis: The Idea of Dance in the Sanskritic Tradition, Springer & Kluwer AcademicPublishers, 1991

Mata Prasad Gupt, Tulsidas, Lokbharti Prakashan, Allahabad, 2002

Milo Cleveland Beach, The Grand Mogul: Imperial Painting in India, Sterling and Francine Clark Art Institute, Massachusetts, USA, 1978

Muhammad Hussain Azad, Urdu Kavya ki Jeevan-dhara, Nagari Pracharini Sabha, Varanasi, First Edition 1979

Mukul Dey, Portraits of Mahatma Gandhi, Orient Longman, 1948

My Life with Kotnis, Manak Publications PVT. Ltd. Delhi, First Edition, 2006

Nancy Cox-McCormack Cushman, Five Weeks in London, England 1931

Nilratan Sen, Early Eastern NIA Versification, Indian Institute of Advanced Study, Simla, First Edition, 1973

Nilratansen Sen, (ed.) Caryagitikosa Indian Institute of Advanced Study, Simla, First Edition, 1977

P.K. Parameshwaran Nair, History of Malayalam Literature,(English Translation from Malayalam by E.M. J. Venniyoor), Sahity Akademi, 1958

Parashuram Chaturvedi (ed.), Mirabai's Padavali, Hindi Sahitya Sammelan, Prayag, Nineteenth Edition, 1993

Percival Spear, Twilight of the Mughals, Cambridge at the University Press, 1951

Plato, Republic, (Tr.C.D.C. Reeve), Hackett Publishing, 2004

Premchand, Playground (Rangbhoomi), Tr. Manju Jain, Penguin India, First Edition 2011

Premlata Sharma, Sahaasras, Sahitya Akademi, New Delhi, First Edition, 1972

R. Siva Kumar, Ramkinkar Baij: A Retrospective, 1906 - 1980, Delhi Art Gallery and the National Gallery of Modern Art, New Delhi, 2012

Radhavallabha Tripathi, Sanskrit Sāhitya ka Abhinav Itihāsa, Vishwavidyalaya Prakashan, Varanasi, First Edition 2001

Rajshekhar, Kavya Mimansa, Bihar Rashtrabhasha Parishad, Patna, Third Edition, 2000

Ramchandra Shukla, Hindi Sahitya ka Itihas, Nagri Pracharini Sabha, Kashi, 1983

Ramnaresh Tripathi, Tulsidas aur unki Kavita, Pahla Bhag, Hindi Mandir Prayag, Pahla Sanskaran, 1937

Ramswaroop Chaturvedi, Hindi Sāhitya aur Samvedana ka Vikas, Lokbharati Prkashan, Allahabad, Pratham Sanskaran, 1986

Ranjit Guha (ed), Subaltern Studies III, Oxford University Press, Delhi, 1984

Rashmi Vajpayee (ed.), Kathak Prasang, Rajkamal Prakashan, Delhi, second edition, 1999

Romain Rolland And Gandhi Correspondence, Publication Division, Delhi, Restored Edition 2017

Sabyasachi Bhattacharya (ed.), The Mahatma and the Poet, National Book Trust, Delhi, second reprint 1999

Sangeeta Datta, Kaustav Bakshi, Rohit K. Dasgupta,(eds.), Rituparno Ghosh: Cinema, Gender and Art, Routledge, New Delhi, London, New York, First Published 2016

Sarangadeva, Sangitaratnakar, Tr.R.K.Shringy and Premlata Sharma, Munshiram Manoharlal, New Delhi, 1991

Sarangdev, Sangeet Ratnakar, Sangeet Karyalaya, Hathras, first edition, 1964

Sarojini Naidu, The Broken Wing, William Heinemann, London, 1917

Satya Graha: Indian and South African Artists' Tribute to the Spirit of 9-11-1906 : Collection of Essays and Catalogue (ed) V. K. Cherian, Jayaram Poduval, Afrikhadi India, Kizo Gallery, Afrikhadi India and Kizo Gallery, Durban, 2006

Sexing the Body, Anne Fausto-Sterling, Basic Books, New York, first edition 2000

Sheldon Pollock (ed.), Literary Cultures in History, University of California Press, Berkley and Los Angeles, California, 2003

Sheldon Pollock. Language of the Gods, Permanent Black, 2006

Shovona Narayan, Kathak, A Shubhi Publication Enterprise, First economy edition, 2012

Shriman Narayan (ed.), The Selected Works Of Mahatma Gandhi, vol.six, Navajivan Publishing House, Ahmedabad, Third Reprint Popular Edition, 1995 Shriman Narayan, Ibid, p.304–305 (Harijan, 14-11-1936)

Shriman Narayan, Ibid, p.289. (Young India, 13.11.1924)

Shyam sundar Das (ed.), Kabir Granthawali, Lokbharti Prakashan, Allahabad, Second Edition 2011

Sisir Kumar Das, A History of Indian Literature, 1911–56, Sahitya Akademi, Delhi, First Published 1995

Sohalnlal Dwivedi (ed.) Gandhi Abhinandan Granth, Gandhi Abhinandan Granth Karyalaya, Lucknow, 1944

Som Prakash Verma, Interpreting Mughal Painting, New Delhi, Oxford University Press,

Sri Aurobindo, The Foundations of Indian Culture, Sri Aurobindo birth centenary library, volumes 14, Sri Aurobindo Ashram, Pondicherry, 1972

Sriseetaramsharan bhagwanprasad roopkala, Shreebhaktamal and Priyadas pranitt Tikka-Kavitt, Tejkumar book depot pvt. Ltd, Lucknow, 2009.

Syed Moazzam Ali (ed.) Nakhlistan, Rajasthan Urdu Academy, Jaipur, 2019.

The Millennium Kabir Vani, Manohar, Delhi, First published 2000

The Orwell Reader, Harcourt Brace and Company, New York, First Edition 1956,

Tripta Verma, Karkhana under the Mughals, From Akbar to Aurangjeb, Pragati Publications, Delhi, First Published, 1994

Tulsidas, Vinaypatrika, Geeta Press, Gorakhpur, fifty-second edition 2000

University of Toronto Press, Toronto, 1999

Vamanrao H. Deshpande, Indian Musical Traditions, Popular Prakashan Private Limited, Bombay, second edition 1987

Vidyanivas Mishra (ed), Bodha Granthavali, Nagri Pracharini Sabha, Varanasi, Pratham sanskaran 1974

Vidyanivas Mishra, Satyadev Mishra (eds), Raskhan Rachnavali, vani Prakashan, Delhi, 1993

Vishwanathprasad Mishra, Gosain Tulsidas, Vani Vitan Prakashan, Varanasi, 1965

W. Foster, (ed.) The Embassy of Sir Thomas Roe to India 1615–19, Munshiram Manoharlal Publishers, Delhi, 1990

W.H. Moreland, India at the death of Akbar, Macmillan and co.London, 1920

Walter Benjamin, Illuminations, Fontana press, 1992

World wide web

- http://www.flickr.com/photos/22955235@N00/1239254680/in/set-72157600028124617

- http://www.livemint.com/Consumer/NGQP6dAn14VkftVnA3FBbL/Filmmaker-Rituparno-Ghosh-49-dies-of-cardiac-arrest.html

- http://mrinalsen.org/neel_akasherr_niche.html

- http://www.firstpost.com/bollywood/an-icon-beyond-labels-man-woman-or-rituparno-830493.html

- http://www.galbithink.org/lessmore.htm

- http://www.youtube.com/watch?v=D01xA03C8yE

- https://en.qantara.de/content/what-muslims-and-christians-share-a-christmas-meditation

- https://www.rottentomatoes.com/m/nightmare_in_red_china

- https://www.saffronart.com/sitepages/articledetails.aspx?articleid=867

- https://www.thehindu.com/books/books-authors/gandhi-in-urdu literature /article 28708422 .ece

- Jahangir Preferring a Sufi Shaikh to Kings, Bichitr (act. 1615–50) India, Mughal period. Opaque watercolor, gold, and ink on paper. Smithsonian Institution, Washington D.C. http://resobscura.blogspot.com/2011/02/jahangirs-turkey-early-modern.html

- Madonna with Infant Jesus, Unattributed, 17th century, Mughal, Prince of Wales Museum of western India.

- http://www.chapatimystery.com/archives/homistan/postcolonial_skins.html

- http://asianart.com/articles/minissale/5.html

- http://en.wikipedia.org/wiki/List of artistic depictions of Mahatma Gandhi

- https://epaper.telegraphindia.com/calcutta/2018-10-21/71/Page-12.html

- https://epaper.telegraphindia.com/calcutta/2018-10-21/71/Page-12.html

- https://m.facebook.com/439885819479987/photos/a.518871624914739/1088951051240124/?type=3&_se_imp=1lYAWdGryZ6uxV03j

- https://scroll.in/article/674358/two-indian-sculptors-have-created-most-of-the-gandhi-statues-around-the-world

- https://timesofindia.indiatimes.com/blogs/plumage/ram-sutar-and-mahatma-gandhi-the-journey-goes-back-to-many-decades/

- https://timesofindia.indiatimes.com/blogs/plumage/tom-vattakuzhys-death-of-gandhi/

- https://www.architecturaldigest.in/content/mahatma-gandhiji-jayanti-artists-delhi-2019/

- https://www.devdiscourse.com/article/arts/211974-mahatma-gandhis-sculpture-features-in-exhibition-at-national-gallery-of-modern-art

- https://www.edexlive.com/happening/2018/sep/27/from-facial-recognition-to-3d-printing-everything-that-went-into-mahatma-gandhis-two-sided-bust-in-4038.html

- https://www.nationalheraldindia.com/india/gandhi-and-bengal-a-complicated-relationsh

- https://www.oneindia.com/2010/11/30/mahatmagandhi-statues-and-busts-popularworldwide. html

- https://www.telegraphindia.com/culture/arts/paresh-maity-painter-of-longest-work-pays-tribute-to-tallest-leader-gandhi/cid/1672816 (accessed on 14.09.2022)

- https://www.theheritagelab.in/elizabeth-brunner-dream-india/

- https://www.thehindu.com/entertainment/art/many-moods-of-the mahatma/ article 29519808.ece

- https://www.thehindu.com/entertainment/art/many-moods-of-the-mahatma/ article29519808. Ece

- https://www.theweek.in/theweek/cover/2019/06/21/assassination-painting-of-gandhi-at-rashtrapati-bhavan-an-exercise-in-myth-making.html

- akbar/europeanart/europeanart.html

- http:// collectionsonline.lacma.org/ mwebcgi/ mweb .exe?request=record;id=37429;type=101

- http://asianart.com/articles/minissale/4.html

- http://www.cbl.ie/cbl_image_gallery/collection/list.aspx?collectionId=2

◄ http://www.columbia.edu/itc/mealac/pritchett/00routesdata/ 1500

◄ http://www.conniemadson.com/artmovements/09%20 islamic%20and%20mughal%20art.html

◄ http://www.davidmus.dk/en/collections/islamic/materials/miniatures/art/6-1981

◄ http://www.indianpost.com/viewstamp.php/Issue%20Date/year/1952/TULSIDA

◄ http://www.mullocksauctions.co.uk/lot-41541 india_%E2%80%93_mughal_painting_of_christ_c18th_century.html

◄ http://www.telegraphindia.com/1101222/jsp/entertainment/story_13330745.jsp

◄ https://epaper.telegraphindia.com/calcutta/2018-10-21/71/Page-12.html

◄ https://scroll.in/magazine/828114/on-stage-in-maharashtra-nathuram-godse-is-seeing-a-revival

◄ https://theprint.in/opinion/heres-how-indian-films-of-the-1930s-and-1940s-used-gandhi-in-their-ads/2 96271/

◄ https://www.architecturaldigest.in/content/mahatma-gandhiji-jayanti-artists-delhi-2019/

◄ https://www.firstpost.com/living/manu-parekhs-canvasses-a-retrospective-spanning-60-years-of-the-artists-work-highlights-his-vitality-4098303.html

- https://www.orfonline.org/expert-speak/gandhi-great-influencer-on-hindi-cinema-despite-his-celluloid-aversion-56035/

- The Deposition from the Cross, Unknown, c.1598, Mughal, Watercolour, Gold, ink on paper, Victoria and Albert Museum, London

- http://www.tribuneindia.com/2005/20051225/spectrum/main2.htm)

- http://en.wikipedia.org/wiki/Saint_Matthew

- http://resobscura.blogspot.com/2011/02/jahangirs-turkey-early-modern.html

- http://www.tribuneindia.com/2005/20051225/spectrum/main2.htm

- https://en.wikipedia.org/wiki/Rituparno_Ghosh

- http://www.columbia.edu/itc/mealac/pritchett/00routesdata/1500_1599/

- www.nowrunning.com

ACKNOWLEDGEMENTS

I wish to acknowledge and thank the following institutions and websites for the figures reproduced in this book:

- ◅ American Institute of Indian Studies, Gurgaon
- ◅ Ashutosh Museum of Indian Art, Calcutta University
- ◅ Bharat Kala Bhavan, Varanasi
- ◅ Chugtai Museum, Lahore
- ◅ Geeta Press, Gorakhpur
- ◅ National Gallery of Modern Art, Delhi
- ◅ National Museum, Delhi
- ◅ Viswa-Bharati University, Shantiniketan

- ◅ http://asianart.com
- ◅ http://en.wikipedia.org/wiki

- ◄ http://resobscura.blogspot.com
- ◄ http://www.livemint.com
- ◄ https://en.qantara.de/content
- ◄ https://scroll.in/magazine
- ◄ https://www.firstpost.com/living/
- ◄ https://www.oneindia.com

www.ingramcontent.com/pod-product-compliance
Lightning Source LLC
Chambersburg PA
CBHW041310120726
48005CB00014B/1941